Weekend Guy

A SURVIVAL GUIDE

written & illustrated by
Vince Grittani

KEY PORTER BOOKS

Canadian Cataloging in Publication Data
Grittani, Vince
    The weekend guy: a survival guide
ISBN 1-55263-045-5
1. Men — Recreation. 2. Vacation homes. 3. Country life. I. Title.

GV191.6.G74 1999   643'.2   C98-932980-1

The publisher gratefully acknowledges the support of the Canada Council for the Arts and the Ontario Arts Council for its publishing program.

Canadä
We acknowledge the financial support of the Government of Canada through the Book Publishing Industry Development Program (BPIDP) for our publishing activities.

Key Porter Books Limited
70 The Esplanade
Toronto, Ontario
Canada M5E 1R2

www.keyporter.com

Electronic formatting: Lightfoot Art & Design Inc.
Design: Peter Maher

Printed and bound in Canada

99 00 01 02 6 5 4 3 2

THE AFTERLIFE

One of the things about appearing on television is that once you have established yourself with a certain image, no matter what you do afterward, viewers continue to think of you as "the guy who …" And although it's been several years since I worked on the series and I have gone on to other projects, people still continue to remind me that I'm "the funny guy from Cottage Life Television, with Pistol the big shaggy dog"… just in case I forgot.

The weekend experience—whether at the cottage, the cabin, the chalet, the bungalow, or simply in the backyard—breaks through all language and regional barriers, making it one of the few truly national elements of the Canadian identity. Over the years I have witnessed many aspects of weekend life, even beyond those on view at the end of my dock. I could just as easily be the hobby farm guy, the yacht guy, the RV guy, the B&B guy, or the outdoor guy. And as distinct as each of these experiences are, I have come to appreciate the strong common elements that bind them together. Like the state of mind that weekend relaxing creates. How far we travel, and *how* we travel. What we eat and how we prepare it. How we look and who we spend our time with.

The Weekend Guy is a title I share with everyone. Anyone, of either sex, with the right attitude can be a weekend guy.

THE WEEKEND SCHOOL OF THOUGHT

"So I'm reading this wall and they predict that some day the sun's rays will actually be harmful. Imagine ... that's like saying some day dinosaurs will be extinct!"

HISTORY 101

Just a Theory

It is common knowledge that God is really the one responsible for initiating the whole weekend thing, by resting on the seventh day; however, it is man who invented the Industrial Revolution and sped things up, therefore creating far too much free time and resulting in the invention of the "weekend"—or as the British say, "week*end*," or the Parisians, "le weekend."

Now, I'm not trying to turn this into a religious or political argument. However, I believe the weekend is built right into our biological clock, that it actually goes back to when we lived in caves and the whole family piled on top of the family sport utility dinosaur and spent a few days relaxing up at the tar pits.

THE WEEKEND DICTIONARY
Speaking Weekendeze!
Part of the whole weekend experience is speaking the lingo, weekendeze. It's a dialect that only weekenders speak and understand, comprised of simple terms, usually with meanings that are applicable to the weekend experience.

Throughout this book you'll find examples that may look and sound familiar, but when spoken within the weekend context they take on a whole new meaning.

Inevitably, by about three o'clock on Sunday afternoon, dad would start getting all irritable because he knew that he would have to drive back to the cave. Then the next morning he'd have to get up and invent the wheel or discover fire.

Of course, everyone was advised not to trade for wheels made on Monday or cook over a fire built on a Friday. And the reason? Workers who made them, their minds … well, were still back at the tar pits.

So the next time you get that funny feeling at about three on a Sunday afternoon and you can't quite figure out why, don't worry. It's just our ancestors talking to us.

It's like nipples on a man. It's just something left over from another era.

WEEKEND PEOPLE

The Weekend Guy: Will That Be Cash or Charge?

Bob Vila. This man can build anything. And the amazing thing is he does it without even picking up a single tool or getting his nails dirty.

He just walks through project after project after project, and you get the impression that he knows what he's talking about and is actually physically participating in the construction of the house, deck or whatever.

6

But what he really knows are a few buzz words. He puts them into a sentence like "Hey Jim, I see that you've installed the TWO BY FOUR," and gives such a great delivery that what you think you've heard is "Now that I have finished installing this TWO BY FOUR, the header is trussed in order to divert some of the weight from above so that it will be carried down to the sill."

And he does this without whacking a thumb, getting a sliver or being forced to stop on account of rain—because in Bob Vila Land a man's nails are manicured, not smashed.

The Weekend Gal: License to Own a Glue Gun

I have two words for you … Martha Stewart. Can you imagine being married to this woman? Not only would your underwear be pressed, it'd be stenciled, silk-

screened and embroidered! And when it got to that nice comfortable stage—you know, soft with a few holes—she would probably take your underwear, cut it into pieces and turn it into a Christmas centerpiece!

But what I don't understand most about Martha Stewart is her audience. Intelligent, educated women who fought against the norm, refused to be like their mothers, built a career, produced the nanny-ed kids, managed their own finances, houses, cars, debts ... And yet they have taken this woman who is Harriet Nelson, Donna Reed and June Cleaver all rolled up in one, placed her on a pedestal somewhere in Connecticut, given her a license to own a glue gun, and now listen to her every word like Stepford wives!

Personally I think Martha needs a little dose of weekend reality. I'd like to see her try gluing her pine cones while chauffeuring the kids to Saturday hockey practice, ballet classes and birthday parties in between grocery shopping for the week ahead, finishing off the big presentation for the new client on Monday morning, plus getting ready for an evening out at a high-school reunion she is being forced to attend ... and then, Ms. Martha Stewart, I wanna hear you say "It's a good thing!"

TEST YOURSELF

Are You a Weekend Guy?

The following test will help you establish if you already are or have the potential of being a weekend guy. There is no cheating, just wishful thinking.

- ☑ Do you suffer from heartburn or any other stress—related symptoms that systematically appear Monday morning at 9:00 a.m. and miraculously disappear Friday at 5:00 p.m.?

- ☑ Do you cringe at the sight of an ivory envelope with fancy script arriving in the mail sometime in May, knowing that it's probably an invitation to a wedding that is going to cut into a prime summer weekend?

- ☑ Do you curse at the building management when trying to park your oversized sport utility vehicle in your downtown underground executive parking spot?

- ☑ Can you justify buying a piece of recreational real estate that will consume 90 percent of your income but that you will be able to enjoy only 20 percent of the time?

- ☑ Do you consider two days of hard labor building a dock "fun" and two minutes of listening to a client whine on the telephone "torture"?

CONT'D ▶

☑ Are you more inclined to answer with enthusiasm to "How was your weekend?" than to "How was your week?"

☑ Does sitting in morning rush hour traffic make you want to say "#@&!" and sitting in Friday night bumper-to-bumper-get-me-to-the-lake traffic make you want to shout "yes!"?

☑ Does your caloric intake increase without guilt on the weekend?

☑ Do you consider your Monday-to-Friday gym workout "training" for a "real" weekend activity?

☑ Do you wish that on the seventh day God had said "Hey, this rest stuff is niiiice," then declared his previous six days of work "a one time only" thing?

If you answered at least one of the above with a yes, then you have potential, and should consider yourself a "w.g.i.t." (wh-ghit, or weekend guy in training). However, if you nodded with recognition at each question, then welcome. You are a full-blooded weekend guy.

How women view
the world

How men view
the world

WEEKEND STYLE

The Weekend Look

Khaki has somehow become the official color of weekend fashion. It's off with the suits and into the "khakis."

You would think we'd go for a color that says, "It's the weekend, I'm letting go." Like banana yellow or fire-hydrant red. No, instead we've adopted a color that says, "I've gone AWOL from the fourth regiment," in styles that let us pretend we are one of Rose Kennedy's lost grandchildren fresh from the Hyannisport family compound.

But then if you really think about it, if anyone has a reputation for "letting go and having fun," it's the Kennedys.

Hmmm … I guess "khaki" is the perfect choice after all.

Weekend Fashion Foibles

Are you one of those people who go away for the weekend and pack a "just-in-case"?

You know what I'm talking about. You arrive dressed in shorts, T-shirt and sandals and cart along a huge bag filled with clothing items, "just-in-case." A good sports jacket, just-in-case you meet the girl of your dreams while out on the lake windsurfing and she happens to be filthy rich and she invites you to her exclusive private club to meet her wealthy father and announce your engagement. Right!

Or do you bring along a bulky sweater, a down jacket and gloves, just-in-case the temperature drops below zero in the middle of July?

Get over it. Stop trying to impress. You're just like everyone else and chances are that come Sunday night you'll still be wearing that same pair of shorts, T-shirt and sandals, and carting back to the city your unopened "just-in-case."

"Don't give me that when-you-were-a-boy scout-and-
always-being-prepared speech. You'll never need your
Armani 'power suit' up at the lake!"

ARE WE THERE YET?

The 4X4 ... Need or Obsession?

A sport utility vehicle: the ultimate weekend car.

Faster than a locomotive, able to leap over rocks and plow through swamps, these vehicles are packed with options rivaling everything from a Sherman tank to a Lincoln Continental ... and yet I ask: Is this a trend driven by need or obsession?

Does one *need* a sport utility vehicle because every weekend leads to an adventure, like mountain-biking the Niagara Escarpment, kayaking the rapids of the mighty Colorado, or skiing the slopes of the Rocky mountains? Or is one *obsessed* with the idea of looking great in khaki and cashmere when plunging through a puddle in the parking lot while grocery shopping on Saturday morning?

My fave is when a married guy purchases The Texas Cadillac, a Suburban, for going up to the cabin on the weekend, and then leaves this 3000-foot vehicle for his 110-pound, 5'5" coiffed wife to scoot around town during the week while he drives his small, imported, sports car, 'cause he claims it's easier to park.

Sounds logical to me.

"This baby has two off-road settings: Overpriced Gourmet Store and Fabulous To-Die-For Antique Shop!"

Weekend Chore Tip: Washing the Car

These days many people prefer to run the auto through the automatic car wash and do away with what I consider one of the most satisfying personal rituals. However, if you have the time, and if you do like participating in this traditional weekend activity, here are a few tips to guarantee your efforts will shine.

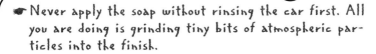

- Never apply the soap without rinsing the car first. All you are doing is grinding tiny bits of atmospheric particles into the finish.

- Don't forget to hose out the wheel wells. Dirt, especially from country roads, can interfere with the efficiency of the brakes.

- Power sprays are great tools; however, if you are using them at the cottage, where the lake is your water source, you run the risk of pitting the paint with tiny minerals that haven't been filtered out.

- It's best to use a soap that contains carnauba, a natural wax, if you don't want to strip off the existing polish. And how do you know it's time to wax? If water stops beading off the surface of the car, then you are ready.

- Finally, washing the car is a great activity and one of the few excuses parents still have for legally hosing down the kids.

Safely Towing Behind the Car

Every day during the summer it amazes me to see how and what people are dragging behind their cars on our highways. Trailers that look as if they are about to break off at any moment, or ones that are totally and dangerously packed. These are the trailers you usually see abandoned on the side of the road.

"Don't worry! This is exactly why they make these vehicles."

Trailer Safety Checkup

☑ The average trailer is used just a couple of times a year, usually to drag everything up at the beginning of the summer season and to drag everything down at the end. Then it's left abandoned to rust in the rain and snow. This is a great way of seizing up the wheel bearings. To prevent this from happening, these bearings should be greased once a season to ensure continuous action.

☑ Directional lights, safety chains and the hitch ball clasp should be checked to see they are working and secure.

☑ Never overload a trailer. Always place the heaviest things, like refrigerators, in the center over the axle.

☑ It's always good to put a tarp over everything. Plus, make sure that items are not only tied down but also tied to avoid sliding back and forth. I find that the nylon straps with the locking winches do the best job.

☑ Finally, don't forget the spare tire. This way you'll never be the one having to leave the trailer on the side of the road.

The Art of Packin'

Unlike packing a suitcase, packing the trailer and car is a fine art that most people are continuously trying to perfect. Many feel that it is an excellent opportunity to practice several principles of new math.

For example, how far can Joe Weekender travel on the highway with one old mattress, a secondhand stove, the neighbors' old BBQ, garden furniture that didn't sell in the garage sale, six old lamps that don't work but are good enough for the cottage, a lawnmower even though the cottage doesn't have grass, plus three tons of junk from the brother-in-law's basement to justify his family staying at your place for a week ... before being pulled over by the police?

The answer? I'd say he'd be lucky if he made it to the city limits.

Driving the Time Away

Whether you are a habitual weekend traveler or setting out on a road vacation, keeping yourself and/or the kids occupied can be a chore.

When traveling alone, my favorite thing is to listen to books-on-tape. I can get through an entire book between the city and the cottage. Many times I have to slow down just so that I can finish the tape.

Traffic jams take on a whole new meaning. I call them intermission. And you don't have to buy the tapes. Most libraries lend them for free.

For the kids, you may consider picking up a combination TV-VCR that plugs into the lighter and fits between the two front seats. Simply add a couple of pairs of earphones and you may never have to turn around and threaten to stop the car again.

Wouldn't that be nice.

DIRECTIONS (n.) dye-wreck-shuns

Giving directions to a weekend retreat can be as much fun as cleaning out the septic system. Maybe it's the reluctance one may feel about telling someone else how to get to their private sanctuary. It's kind of like giving out the combination to a safe and hoping the user forgets it once they get in.

On the other hand, there are those weekenders who give out their directions with great enthusiasm, not forgetting a single detail, so as to make their guests' journey the beginning of one continuous vacationing experience. These are also the people likely to be caught telling the most popular weekend lie—"My place is less than two hours from the city"—completely eliminating the one hour it takes to get out of the city and the half-hour drive on the rough road in off the highway.

"I don't care how many trips it's seen,
I'm buying you a new road map."

THE WEEKEND RETREAT

A weekend retreat can manifest itself in a whole variety of ways, shapes and sizes. From the Kennedy compound Hyannisport (which defeats the whole purpose of getting away from family), to fishing camps in Manitoba, to weathered cottages on the beaches of Prince Edward Island, to even my cousins Anita and Gerry's yacht on Lake Ontario (which spends most of its time on dry-dock under repair, giving my father, a retired mechanic, something to do).

The weekend retreat is usually found in a rural setting but is not always a building designed for residential use. Sometimes it is a structure that is magically transformed under the spell of a visionary. For instance, my friend Robert Gage, hairdresser to the rich and famous, took a typical country church and turned it into an old English manor right out of the play *Sleuth*.

And my friend Linda Hill-Giffin's talented eye metamorphosed a nineteenth-century Ontario farmhouse into a French country chateau. I've seen school houses, train stations, lighthouses, boathouses, mills, hotels and children's camps all take on a new life as someone's private weekend retreat. As unique as these retreats appear, they share much in common with the more popular cottage or chalet. They are all "investments" that like to suck your bank accounts dry!

Yes, my friend, it's time for a reality check. Experiencing a weekend retreat can be the best of times and the worst of times. My intention is to help you make it the best.

To Buy or Not to Buy!

"Somehow this wasn't quite what I imagined
when I was thinking hobby farm."

People are constantly asking me if buying a recreational property is a good investment. Not being a financial advisor I can only speak for myself. Yes, I believe it is a good investment.

Simply put, there is an aging population out there with good incomes, who stand to inherit gazillions of dollars over the next fifteen years, and they, like myself, love the country atmosphere.

So, the demand is there and will remain for several years.

Next, let's talk supply.

Unless God plans on coming out of retirement as a land developer, there are not going to be any more prime lakes, mountains, streams or properties with a great view suddenly created. Also, the number of recreational lots allowed through subdividing is restricted by local municipalities.

This leads us to conclude that …

Supply is decreasing.

Now that people are working from home or portable offices using computers, faxes, the Internet and cell phones, conducting business in your shorts from the end of a dock is no longer a fantasy. It's a reality.

It's a year-round lifestyle.

Finally, the weekend retreat, be it cottage or farm, is more than just a summer lifestyle. Canadians have finally learned to embrace all seasons. (It's about time.) The rise in popularity of winter activities such as cross-country skiing and snowmobiling is more than just a passing fad. These things also make recreational properties that were previously impossible to get to in the winter accessible all year round. So in answer to everyone's question …

Yes, I believe the weekend retreat is a good investment.

Of course, you have to remember that unlike money locked in a mutual fund, you will also be enjoying the property from the time you purchase it. I prefer diving off a dock to watching my money do it on Bay Street.

Okay, now that we have established that a weekend retreat is a good investment how does one decide which property to buy?

Like real estate anywhere, the three most important words are location, location, location.

In addition, there's the factor of driving time involved. Like a successful movie, two hours is the magic number. Of course, there's always the *Titanic* exception. However, the "desired" traveling time still remains two hours. Keep in mind that your location in the city may add up to another hour of travel, which may influence the potential cottage location you will want to explore.

Established areas such as Muskoka and Georgian Bay out of Toronto, Whistler out of Vancouver, and Montreal's Mont Tremblant and Eastern Townships will remain desirable and retain their value.

However, year-round weekend retreats will always be more expensive, and if money is limited, you may try looking at an unwinterized building on a winter-accessible road. This way you can always get the location now and renovate the building as your bank account allows.

d'Islands, Mahn

As diverse as Canadians are, so too are the types of weekend retreats that exist in Canada, from the more populated communities to isolated islands. Speaking of which … Owning or renting a cottage on an island has both advantages and disadvantages.

If you are starting from scratch, building a new structure is generally more expensive than on the mainland. Buying an existing island cottage can be cheaper.

However, you've got to love boating because not only is it a form of entertainment, it is your primary mode of transportation. When you arrive on a Friday night you still have to unload the car, load up the boat, drive to the island and unload the boat before you can relax.

You also have to plan more when it comes to grocery shopping and arranging for the arrival of deliveries or guests. But a weekend retreat on an island is much more private and does discourage people from just dropping in.

Depending on the distance from the mainland, wildlife may be less and the winds greater, which results in the one single reason why island cottaging is so appealing: less or no mosquitoes and blackflies.

Need I say more?

"Now here's a place that some people say is overbuilt. I, on the other hand, feel that they have maximized the potential."

"Why me? I'm not really sure, except that weekends are the only thing every Canadian has no matter what."

The Identity Question

Yes, the cottage is something that Canadians have embraced as part of our lore and our culture from coast to coast. Not that this lifestyle doesn't exist elsewhere, it's just that no one else has embraced it with such ... well, emotion.

I think it has to do with the fact that in our mobile society, where it's nothing for family members to pick up and move across the country and where Mom and Dad move out of the house we grew up in and into a condo, the cottage is a symbol of emotional stability.

A cottage is the one place to which you can return and find your initials still carved on a tree. The neighbors may not be the same, but at least they are probably the children of the couple you knew growing up.

And then there are the cottage communities that represent our ethnic and economic diversity. In a way, going up to the cottage every weekend is not just a family matter, it's part of our Canadian identity.

HEY, BUT WHAT ABOUT RENTING?

Each year I am bombarded in the middle of July by friends asking if my place is available for rent. They are "desperate," they claim.

"Remember this feeling and avoid the rush," I answer back.

Although I am going to use "the summer cottage" as the rental example here, my advice is very similar for renting out a winter chalet or any other type of weekend retreat. And before I begin, let me just tell you that looking around at the last minute only leaves you with limited choice and your wallet empty. Also, I think renting before buying is a good idea when you have more than one accessible recreational area to choose from. This allows you to taste various regional "cultures."

Yeah, But What Do I Want?

Like all things in life, deciding what you actually want when making a decision can be the hardest thing about making the decision. So, to help you out, here are a few guidelines ...

The Butt Factor!

Again, as when purchasing a property, the clock rules. However, when renting, you have more flexibility with the timing/distance factor because you are more likely to tolerate a longer ride as a one-time deal than for the next twenty-five years of your life. But when renting, you have to decide the length of your stay before considering distance, for it will definitely influence things like price and the length of time you can be without other necessities like cable, your relatives and instant access to the Internet.

If you are planning on renting for a season, chances are that you'll be doing a lot of traveling back and forth to the city. So keep in mind the two- to two-and-a-half-hour travel-time tolerance level. Besides the similarity to the length of time you can watch a movie without your butt going to sleep, this is also a scientifically obtained calculation that I have come up with, factoring in bladder size, ability to sit and listen nonstop to your friend Mitzie in a contained space without committing murder, plus the length of time you can go without having to act upon that age-old threat "If you kids don't settle down ..."

However, if you are planning on renting for a set block of time, like a month or a few weeks, and will not be running back to the city every few days to hold your client's hand, then a one-time three-and-a-half to five-hour journey is quite tolerable; it gives you more choice and is more likely to take you out of the "you-won't-believe-for-how-much-I-can-rent-my-dump-of-a-cottage" zone.

My Needs ...

Next, you have to establish your "needs" according to the number in your party. If you are single or just a couple, then your needs are likely going to be less expansive than, say, if you were a large Irish Catholic family like actress Catherine O'Hara's. This will influence the number of bedrooms, the type of terrain (beachfront, cliffs, etc.), and closeness to town and other activities, especially if you have teenagers who are embarrassed to be seen with you.

The best way to help figure out needs is to visualize an entire day from dusk to dawn and the activities in which you and your party will most likely want to participate—like swimming, boating and the all-important shopping. Don't forget to allow yourself choices, for odds are you won't be able to match all your needs.

While you are on the floor in that lotus position here are a few additional questions that you may want to ask yourself:

What can I afford?

This is where sharing with a friend or relative enters the picture.

What is my purpose?

I'm not asking a life question here but rather are you looking to be waited upon or are you looking to work. This of course will influence who you decide to rent with, and maybe eliminate people like your unemployed brother-in-law.

What is important?

Are you into "rustic living," like no indoor plumbing and using an outhouse, or are you a wimp who can't live without a cappuccino maker? Are you into smacking waves in a personal watercraft, or singing old camp songs with your paddle "flashing with silver" as you dip, dip and swing along a serene, undisturbed lake?

Answering all these questions in advance will assist you when quizzing any future owner about a potential rental property and reduce those unexpected surprises.

The Trek ... In Search of Dock

Once you have decided what you want you are ready to begin your search. But remember, *one person's paradise can be another person's hell.* So keep your ears open and ask a lot of questions.

There are several ways of looking for a rental property, but the one I recommend most is word-of-mouth. There is nothing like a satisfied renter to advertise a great vacation property. Begin by asking your friends if they have rented a place they would recommend. If you don't have any luck there you can trying putting a notice on the bulletin board at work.

If word of mouth doesn't give you any leads it is time to begin the leg work. I suggest you get a map and, using your home as a center, draw a circle encompassing the area you are willing to travel. For example, if you live in Toronto and are looking for a place you can use every weekend for an entire season, using two and a half hours as your guideline will see your circle reach Huntsville to the north, Lake Erie to the west, east to Prince Edward County and south to upstate New York.

Now that you have a point of reference, you can move to the next step of actually looking. Most major newspapers include a seasonal rental section in the classifieds. Usually the ads identify where the cottage is located so you can immediately refer to your map and decide if it is in your desired travel zone.

Another way of searching is by purchasing a recreational property-rental directory—like the *Cottage Rental Guide*, which is published once a year—or looking on the Internet.

With all of these methods you are dealing directly with the owner and should be able to get firsthand details. But remember, owners are as different as the places they are trying to rent. Some are desperate and will embellish the truth. Others will be selective and may interrogate you, which is understandable considering you are a total stranger. A cottage is a person's second home.

A third way of looking is through an agent. There are several companies that do nothing but rent out recreational properties. The good thing here is that you are more than likely going to get an honest description of the place, since their reputation is on the line. You'll also get a contract, which most individuals are unlikely to give and which you can use if, God forbid, something goes wrong.

And When You Finally Find Paradise ...

Here are a few examples of the types of questions you may want to ask:

How long have they been renting out the cottage or chalet?

This may give you insight as to their experience at dealing with renters.

While traveling through Nova Scotia in the summer of '98 I visited my cousin Lisa and her husband Paul, who had rented a place near Lunenburg. They were not happy campers. The picture of the cottage they had been faxed was not the same cottage they had rented. There was no gas BBQ as advertised, and the beach that was "right across the road" was actually a couple of kilometers away. When questioned by Paul later, the owner used the excuse that it was her first time renting.

Nice excuse, eh!

Are there extra costs?

For instance, if the property is not road accessible, does one have to pay to park at the local marina?

Is it on the lake or near a lake?

How close are the neighbors?

What is included when they say "kitchen"?

Hopefully more than a hotplate.

What is included in the bathroom facilities?

Remember, a cottage bathroom can be an outhouse, with the lake to bathe in.

Is there a boat you can use?

Can you have guests?

What are the beds like?

Singles, doubles, bunks?

Do they have a TV, CD player, etc.?

Lifesavers on a rainy day.

Do they provide linens?

Do they provide cleaning services?

When you finally find something over the telephone that suits all your needs, whenever possible try to get up and see the place. In some cases you may have to hike in through knee-high snow. Not only will this make a nice midwinter outing, but it will provide you with peace of mind before you hand over a single cent.

If visiting is not possible, ask to see photos or videos. And I guess, based on Lisa and Paul's experience, ask to be assured that they are of the rental property in question, not some reasonable facsimile.

Expect in all cases, especially when renting in popular areas like Muskoka or Whistler, to pay in full at the time of booking. You may be asked to pay a refundable security deposit depending on the individual cottage and costs involved.

Finally ... as a Renter

Here are a couple of unwritten rules that one should follow when renting out any recreational property at any time of the year, especially if it is privately owned.

Respect the place as if it's your own.

Remember, you are probably renting a private cottage or chalet from someone who is doing it to cover expenses. If you like the place and want to return I suggest you take care. Like guests from hell you won't be allowed back.

Numbers count.

When you say party of five stick to five. If you want to have more ask the owners. Don't let them find out about your big bash from the irate neighbors.

All isn't included.

There is nothing more annoying than getting your cottage phone bill and discovering long-distance calls that you didn't make. Don't forget to use your calling card or cell phone. And if you go into a private food or beer stock, please don't forget to replace it.

Finally (and this time I mean it) ... respect the septic tank!

Ask anyone who has a rural property and they'll tell you how delicate the septic system can be. I'll never forget that hot weekend in August when, after having rented the cottage out for July, I was forced to dig up a sewer pipe clogged with Tampax and toilet paper. Never again!

Renting Out

Have you ever thought of renting out your weekend retreat, maybe to cover the taxes or the high costs of feeding your brother-in-law? It can be a profitable venture if you do it right.

Actually, take everything I have said about renting a weekend retreat and reverse it.

First, if you are afraid of renting to absolute strangers, then put a notice up at work or just tell your friends. You'll be surprised by the number of responses you'll get.

When you've got someone interested, don't be afraid of asking nosy questions like:

- Is this their first time renting?
- How many people, children and adults?
- Are they planning on having guests?
- Do they have pets?
- Are they bringing up toys, like boats or snowmobiles?

Let them know what they can use, especially when it comes to boats, spas and other equipment. Your insurance may not cover renters and you may be liable if anything happens.

Be very specific about when they can arrive and when they have to leave. If you are not, this can cause problems if you have new renters following them.

When it comes to price, think about this: Where can you take a family of four for an eight-hundred-dollar-a-week vacation. Use this as your base figure and work around it.

"Actually, the agent is telling the truth.
It does have a view of the lake ... from here."

THE WEEKEND DICTIONARY

VIEW (n.) veehew

"What a view!" are a weekender's three most valuable words. A view is strictly a personal thing and reflects directly back to the character of the weekender. Some people choose a calm, serene view that makes them forget about the rest of the world, while others prefer a view that is constantly reminding them that they are not alone. A perfect panoramic picture from one's precious property can practically preserve the present price of any person's playground, palatial or primitive. But any alteration to this view can permanently prevent the possibility of profiting at any promising proposition.

AN OUNCE OF PREVENTION:
BEING PREPARED

Opening Up a Seasonal Retreat

Opening up a seasonal cottage or cabin can be one of the most exciting annual events. However, to avoid turning it into a disaster here are a few tips:

- Before turning on the hydro, make sure the hot water tank is off to prevent burning out the element. The tank has to have water in it or else. This is a common mistake and is very profitable for the local hardware store.

- Before unpacking or making beds, check all cupboards, closets, beds and furniture, and get ready to clean up any evidence of tiny critters who moved in over the winter. As a precaution, always wear rubber gloves and even a face mask when doing the cleanup.

- Don't forget to put fresh batteries into all the smoke detectors.

- Finally, don't try to accomplish everything in the first weekend. Sometimes we forget that we are at the cottage to relax.

Waterfront Safety Check

So you've put the dock in the water, you've launched the boat, and now all that's left is to sit back and enjoy. Let me just say, in those famous words of the Carpenters ... "You've only just begun."

Now it's time to safety proof your waterfront.

☑ First thing is a cleanup of all the debris the ice left for you during the spring melt, including the front end of your neighbor's dock. I suggest you do a manual check, in the water, wearing a pair of waterproof shoes.

☑ Then the dock itself needs to be looked over. Get rid of any slippery algae with a wire brush or by using a biodegradable wash.

☑ Check for nails, especially on the surface. They tend to pop with movement or seasonal shifting. And at the same time sand down any splinters that may have developed.

☑ Finally, something many people never do is equip their dock area with safety gear. The most important thing is keeping within clear view of everyone some sort of reaching device, like a pole or even better an empty plastic jug with a cap, half-full of water and tied to a twenty-foot rope. Learn how to use it properly. As a rule you should never stand when pulling someone to safety. Remember, it's better to be prepared than sorry.

Fireproofing the Cabin

It's always a good thing to give the cottage or cabin a thorough fire-safety checkup, both at the beginning and the end of the season.

- ✔ First of all, test all the batteries in the smoke detectors. And if you still haven't installed them now is the best time.
- ✔ If you have a fireplace or woodstove, especially if you haven't used it in a while, check the chimney to ensure that no animal has been nesting up there.
- ✔ Also, you may want to give the stack a cleanout, removing any creosol that could cause a chimney fire.
- ✔ Check that all the fire extinguishers are charged and easy to get at.
- ✔ Outside, look to see that leaves or wood is not piled up against the exterior of the building or underneath if the crawlspace is not enclosed.
- ✔ All flammable chemicals such as kerosene or gas for the boat should be stored in a separate shed or building away from the main structure.
- ✔ Make sure that you have planned in advance more than one escape route and method in case of a fire, especially if you have a second floor.
- ✔ And finally, take the time to visit your local fire department for further information on how you can keep your weekend retreat fireproof.

Avoiding the Shock of Your Life!

I want to talk to you about avoiding the shock of your lifetime. No, not your tax bill, but lightning.

There is really nothing more exciting and, some even think, romantic than a storm up at the lake. Listening to the rain pelt down on the roof or counting the seconds after a flash in the sky until the thunder erupts is all part of the fun. But I must pass on a warning from my own experience.

In today's high-tech society, lightning in the country can be your worst enemy. Many, including myself, have introduced to our weekend retreats equipment like VCRs, digital telephones and computers—all of which are prime targets for electrical surges when lightning strikes.

"Hey Pete, watch me knock out this guy's VCR, computer, cappuccino maker and satellite dish in one shot!"

Last summer during a huge storm, lightning hit the telephone poles, sending a surge of electricity into the cottage and frying both my modem on the computer and the VCR, even though both were supposedly grounded and plugged into a power-surge bar.

What precautions can one take to avoid such a mishap? Properly installed lightning rods are a possibility but not a guarantee, and are only useful if placed higher than the telephone and power lines.

Your best bet to avoid frying all your high-tech toys is to never leave the equipment plugged into either a power or telephone outlet.

On the other hand, maybe lightning is God's way of telling us to leave our high-tech stuff at home.

Concepticulizing ... Avoiding It from Hitting the Fan

Now I want to talk to you about something that anyone who owns a place in the country, be it chalet, cottage or hobby farm, holds sacred.

No, I'm not talking about the view, I am talking about the septic system. People don't realize that a septic system is like a loving relationship: you say it's forever, but if you don't pay attention to it, it will block you out.

Given the fact that a cottage or chalet is used seasonally, having the tank cleaned out every two years will probably be sufficient. Because the system relies on anaerobic bacteria to function properly, flushing a mixture of yeast down once a season will also help keep things running smoothly.

And finally, the septic bed is *not* a good place to park cars. However, the odd inebriated guest has been known to fall asleep on it.

Cottage Security

Keeping the cottage, farmhouse or cabin in the woods secure when you are not there has always been a difficult task. Even a modern alarm system is only as good as the response time of the police or other security forces, which can be long in some cases … especially if you are on an island. But there are a few preventative steps that you can take to deter a potential break-in.

First, out of sight is out of mind. Make sure all windows have some sort of covering that prevents window shopping and easy viewing of contents.

Second, switches with timers and motion detectors can give the illusion that someone is at home or nearby.

And finally, since alcohol is the most common thing stolen from a cottage or chalet, which sign is going to do the job? One announcing that the property is electronically monitored by some company several miles away, or a posted notice at all entrances proclaiming that for religious reasons alcohol is not allowed in your house? Hey, they're thieves. It's okay to lie to them.

ATTENTION THIEVES: All alcohol and electronic equipment has been removed. So, it is otherwise a futile effort to break in. Thanks.

THiNGS THAT GO BUMP: GUESTS, BUGS AND OTHER SUCH THiNGS

What Is a Weekend Guest?

The weekend retreat guest, not to be confused with the house guest of the same species, is in a category of its own.

Basically, they are divided up into two groups: invited and uninvited. The invited, or welcome weekend guest, is usually someone to whom you extend a formal invitation. The guest responds eagerly, asking when they should arrive, what they can bring and generally how they can be of assistance to you in order to make the weekend experience pleasant for everyone.

The uninvited, or unwelcome weekend guest, can originate as an invited one, but can quickly switch categories. Criteria for identifying an uninvited guest is quite simple:

ONE, if they show up unannounced without any groceries, linens or towels.

TWO, if they show up and complain about the rustic conditions and lack of service. Or

THREE, if they do manage to bring along a case of beer, and it doesn't get opened, they take it back home— because you obviously had enough in your own supply.

How to Invite Guests to Your Weekend Retreat

The best way to learn how to invite a guest for the weekend is to learn how *not* to invite them.

Okay, here is a scenario for you … Johnny Leisure is inviting his friends Sam & Mary Freeloader up to his cottage for the weekend.

Mary answers the phone and Johnny says, "Hello Mary, this is Johnny. Would you and Sam like to come up to my cottage this weekend?"

Question: Is this the wrong way or right way?

Answer: Wrong.

It would be right if Johnny wanted to wait on Sam and Mary hand and foot all weekend long. So how do you invite someone up to the cabin and at the same time let them know exactly what is expected of them?

It's simple, if you keep in mind the following rules.

Never beg!

An over-enthusiastic host, even though it may not be their intention, will make the invitees think they are doing the host a favor. Remember, the favor is *the host's.*

Try something like this …

"I had a cancellation this weekend and I recall you telling me a couple of years ago that you wanted to come up. Speaking of coming up, your name did appear on my waiting list …"

Keep a list!

Let them know that it's a *privilege* to be a weekend guest. Now, indicate exactly what they should bring. Remember, your intention is to get them to stock up your place with as many supplies as possible *without them realizing what you are doing.*

Food!

Tell them you'll take care of the Friday and Sunday dinners and they can take care of Saturday's. Since everyone will be stuffed with roadside burgers on Friday night, you'll only have to take care of Sunday's meal. But if you are clever you can get out of that one too. Tell them "I insist that you stay right to Sunday night. Of course, if you leave early enough you'll avoid the traffic jams going home ..." This should clear you.

Your next move is to get the guests to bring non-perishables that you need and are sure they'll leave behind.

"You may want to bring, ahhh ... a few lawn chairs." People always leave lawn chairs. And towels.

Remember, if it wasn't for forgetful guests, how else would you stock up on linen? But these are only some of the things that guests can supply.

Here are a few more things that guests love to leave behind:

- Bathing suits
- Suntan lotion
- Half-read novels and magazines
- Tupperware and any other containers used to transport food
- Toys, especially the type left on the beach
- And of course, tapes and CDs

Once you become an expert at getting your guests to supply you with these items, with a little work you can graduate up to big-ticket things like chainsaws and fishing gear.

So remember, a properly invited weekend guest is a guest who keeps on giving *well after they have left.*

Gifts for Weekenders

To all of those out there who may be visiting a weekend retreat this summer or attending the birthday party of a cottage owner, or who have been offered the use of someone's place without them being there, it's most likely that you are going to be presenting your host with a gift. Play it safe when giving a "weekender" gift.

Cash is always welcome, to pay for damage you did to the boat last summer. Or a bottle of wine that *doesn't* have to be mixed with ginger ale to hide the taste.

Let me save you some trouble and embarrassment. Avoid ...

- BBQ aprons that say anything, because just about everything witty has been said before
- ugly candlestick holders that someone gave to you but you think they'd be okay for a cottage
- cute plaques with sayings for the bathroom
- yet another copy of the photographic coffee table book on the lake
- sweat and T-shirts with dumb messages that are meaningless after the occasion
- an additional set of tacky plastic beverage glasses that retain the taste of whatever was last served in them

"We're heeeere. Traffic was murder. Geez, the bugs are bad.
We forgot to go shopping... So, when do we eat?"

Guests from Hell

"What are you doing this weekend? Why don't you come up to the cottage!" or cabin ... or chalet ... or farm. These are the words that can turn a relatively normal human being into a "guest from hell."

Not all guests experience this metamorphosis, but what is it that makes some people think that an invitation to your own private retreat is an invitation for them to be your master? Showing up with no food, expecting to be waited on hand and foot, not even offering to wash a dish, bitching about how it's so quiet they can't sleep, then finally signing your guest book with the sweetest words, hinting for an invite back!

And over the next year you mellow out and for some reason you invite them back. A second chance. They must have changed ... and they *still* don't offer to help, and they *still* bitch! Well, once burned, twice a schmuck!

The Weekend Pooch

Have your holidays ever gone to the dogs?

Well, if your canine companions are anything like my bearded collies Pistol and Cloud, you're not even allowed to *think* of leaving them at home or in a kennel when going on holiday. Actually, ask anyone with a dog and they'll probably tell you the same thing.

Whether you are going south, camping or up to the cottage, dogs love to get away too. But before you leave, don't forget a trip to the vet for shots and especially heart worm pills during the warmer months.

When traveling in the car, work in a regular pit stop so the pooch can relieve himself, even if you don't need to yourself.

It's taken years and laws to ensure that society accepts seat belts. But what about Fido? What's protecting him from becoming a canine projectile in the unfortunate event of a collision? For his safety and yours I suggest a seatbelt chest harness anchored always in the back seat of a car or the rear area of a 4X4 or van. As tempting as it is to allow your pooch to sit freely in the front seat, it is fate that you are really tempting.

"Yes, I put everything away. Now, if we don't hurry, we won't make it home for '60 Minutes.'"

When your get to your campsite or cottage, remember that for a city pup it's a whole new world of scents, smells and aromas which can lead them to your neighbors or out into the forest. Take them around on the leash first and don't let them run wild.

And most of all, you may think you're alone but remember a bark travels far and fast across a calm and peaceful lake.

The Buzzzzzzzzz!

What's the first question most people ask when you invite them to your cottage or cabin for the weekend? "How are the bugs?"

To me, bugs aren't an issue or problem. The question is not how to get rid of them but rather how to live with them. Hey! Let's face it, they were here a long time before we arrived and will remain a long time after we are gone.

Mosquitoes are my favorite bug, because not only do they provide great conversation openers—like "Bugs are bad this year, eh!"—they are also a form of entertainment. There is nothing like sitting in the screened-in porch at dusk watching an air show provided by a squadron of bats diving and eating the little pests by the thousands.

I Could Just Screen!

Soon after the May 24th weekend, the air is inevitably filled with the melodic sounds of slapping and, less frequently, cries of "Gotcha." Tiny little vampire-like creatures try to suck the blood from our still virgin arms, legs, faces and anywhere else they can land on us undetected.

We run for shelter into our homes and screened-in porches only to discover that the bugs have made it in through holes the dog created last fall by scratching to get out and chase a passing chipmunk. You yell out, "I could just scream!" And so you do.

However, there are quick fixes to your problems.

- Tiny holes in nylon screen can easily be fixed by dabbing them with epoxy glue.

- Larger rips can be sewn neatly using nylon thread.

- Holes in metal screens can be quickly repaired with a square piece of screen that measures one inch longer than the actual puncture. Then you pull off four threads from each side and bend the tiny edges upward to a 90 degree angle. Place the square against the hole, feeding the edges through. On the other side, simply bend down the ends, locking the square in place and all those tiny little bugs outside where they belong. This will give you peace of mind, at least until the next time the kids leave the house and you have to let loose with those famous words ...

"Shut the *&%*!* screen door!"

For the Purist

Deet, found in the best commercial repellents, is still the most efficient way of keeping mosquitoes and black flies away. Used under normal conditions it is not harmful. However, it can cause an allergic reaction on some sensitive skin types and on small infants and toddlers.

Instead of deet-based repellents, try washing the exposed body parts with a citronella-and-water mixture. Citronella is available at your local health-food store.

And don't forget the pooch: dogs are major meals for hungry mosquitoes. They too have very sensitive skin. A neckerchief dipped in pure citronella not only makes dogs smell great but keeps them bite-free.

Citronella, the natural way to say "Bug off!"

"Oh look, honey. What an original gift to give. A wonder-ful COFFEE TABLE book on THE LAKE. Who would have ever thought of this?"

THE RULES OF THE GAME

Weekend Rules

I love to entertain at my weekend retreat. There is nothing more exciting than having a group of friends up, listening to great tunes and dancing around the kitchen making one of those communal meals. On the other hand, I am just as happy to be alone on the weekends. Just me, a fine bottle of wine and a great book.

When I first bought my cottage it was amazing how popular I suddenly became. People who I hadn't spoken to in years were calling, rekindling the friendship and fishing for an invite. It was then and there that I established the "golden weekend rules."

First, I have discovered that making plans months in advance is useless. Things come up. Weddings, work and winning the lottery. So the most advance notice I give is one week. Yup—week-to-week invites. Take 'em or leave 'em.

Rule # 1: "Live weekend to weekend!"

This doesn't mean that I am rushing around every weekend to make arrangements for the next. No-siree. Like I said, I like having guests, don't *need* them.

Rule # 2: "Listen to your instinct!"

You hold the cards. You are in control. It's your place. You pay the mortgage and taxes and you can have guests when you feel like it. So don't be bullied or made to feel guilty. Invite who you want when you want.

Rule # 3: "Always tell the truth!"

I tell everyone the same thing. If you want to visit just call and ask … but you better be prepared for the truth. Meaning, if I have a full house and there's no room, or if I just want to be alone, the answer is, "Not this weekend." Most people accept this. However, there are some who just don't get it. No matter what you say they keep insisting on coming, responding with "That's okay, I'll sleep on the couch … or on the dock … or in the barn … or in my car."

Or there are those who guarantee that they'll remain so quiet you'll never even know that they have arrived. No matter what you say, they always have a comeback.

And so that brings me to …

Rule # 4: "Lie if you must!"

In cases like this don't be afraid to lie, but if you are going to sway from the truth do it with gusto. Come up with something to which they *cannot* respond. Say something like, "This weekend? Sorry, but I'm entertaining the president, and well, with the bodyguards and all, there just isn't room. And I wouldn't bother arriving unannounced because the orders are shoot to kill."

THE WEEKEND DICTIONARY
SEPTIC BED (n.)
'ceptik bhead

Usually located next door to the garden bed, the septic bed has long been the cause of both soothing comfort and total distress to weekenders. It is flat and firm, and unlike other beds in the cabin, little action occurs around it, except for the odd badminton game. And although one doesn't kneel down to pray beside the septic bed, more than one weekender has been seen crying over it when it comes time to pay for its replacement.

Allocating Duties to Guests without Guilt!

I know how difficult it can sometimes be to ask a guest to pitch in up at the cottage or chalet. You feel guilty, as if you have no right to ask them to lift a finger.

Hello! Guilt, my friend, doesn't do the shopping before they come up or clean the joint when they are on their way home. Where was guilt that weekend in the early spring when you opened up the place all by yourself?

So you wanna get over this guilt thing? Take a moment and recall the time you slipped into the freezing water while setting up the docks, spent a day and a half trying to get the water pump to work, or filled your lungs with soot while cleaning out the chimney. Now keep these thoughts and just try to say, "Relax, there's nothing to do." Betch'ya can't!

"Apparently they did it to make Goldie feel more at home."

House Rules

You are probably wondering what the difference is between Weekend Rules and House Rules. It's simple, actually.

The host follows Weekend Rules when inviting guests. The guest follows House Rules when accepting the invitation. Some hosts think that establishing House Rules is rather uncouth, or they are afraid to spell them out upon the guest's arrival. However, one must realize that by laying down the law one is actually assisting the guest in avoiding any future embarrassment.

Most guests are from the city and most weekend retreats are in the country. Don't think of House Rules as something that restricts a guest's experience. Think of House Rules as part of your guest's *learning* experience. If spelling out these rules is not your style, relax and just hand them this book opened to this page.

House Rules are going to vary from weekend retreat to weekend retreat. Ski chalets in the winter require different considerations than beach houses in the summer. But in spite of the obvious differences there are common rules that work across the board.

When faxing the directions to new guests you may want to add at the bottom of the page, "You want beer, bring it. You want wine, bring it. You want steak, bring it. You want clean towels & sheets, bring 'em."

Some may feel that this is a little too direct, but just remember this rule the next time on Sunday night when you are loading up the car with empties and dirty laundry. Think of it in the lyrical styling of Leonard Cohen: "I am not a hotel."

Of course, no one wants to restrict a guest's fun and not allow them to play with the toys you have collected over the years. But some guests, especially those not accustomed to roughing it in the country, seem to think that these toys run on air and don't require fuel.

Here's a rule I find very helpful, and it makes a lovely addition as a plaque on the dash of any boat, personal water craft or snowmobile. "He who driveth payeth for gas."

Plumbing at any weekend retreat always seems to be a mystery to any guest. Now that drinking bottled spring water is all the rage, it's not as necessary to remind guests that drinking the water from the lake could possibly result in the growth of a third arm.

However, when it comes to potty-training weekend guests, I find that most need constant reminding. Over the years I have read quite a few witty and even poetic sayings posted on the wall next to toilets at various cottages, farmhouses, cabins, chalets and anywhere else that one might find a septic tank, all attempting to instruct users about the dos and don'ts of using the facilities. For instance, "If it's yellow, let it mellow. If it's brown, flush it down." Charming as this may sound, I find that it is rather ambiguous and could still cause confusion. I prefer the direct approach: "Don't flush anything into the septic that you wouldn't flush through yourself!"

THE WEEKEND DICTIONARY

CRITTERS (n.)
krhit—urs

Similar to relatives, a family of critters can arrive without notice, expect you to feed them and destroy the place in a matter of hours. Not necessarily hostile, critters are only looking to share the great outdoors, something that is rightfully theirs to begin with. Unlike relatives, critters are not as easily tricked, and excuses like "we are full this weekend," "the place is rented out" or "Great! I can use the help, there's lots of work to do!" will not discourage their arrival.

You know you are going too far when...

you start taking your guest's requests literally when asked for a smooth 'lager' at the end of the dock.

WEEKEND ETIQUETTE:
WATCHING YOUR P'S & Q'S, DOTTING YOUR I'S AND GENERALLY COVERING YOUR BUTT!

Negotiating Your Way Out of a Weekend Wedding

Why is it that most people insist on getting married on a weekend? And not just any weekend but on the weekend they think the weather is going to be best. How dare they?

Since weddings usually happen indoors, under a roof, doesn't it make sense to choose a weekend where it's most likely going to snow or rain—*not* when it's sunny and eighty degrees, and when a lot of your guests would rather be up at the cabin or out sailing?

No, instead the happy couple insists on having a "midsummer wedding" just when the fish are jumpin' and the mosquitoes and blackflies have finally left.

Look, I propose a law. Weddings can happen any weekend between Thanksgiving right up to, say, April Fools Day. Excluding, of course, long weekends, and of course dates are susceptible to change at the last minute if excellent ski conditions occur. Then, the rest of the year, all weddings must be held after 5 p.m. between Monday and Thursday.

However, if the five-day forecast predicts rain on the upcoming week-end, you may at the last minute switch it to that weekend.

Now, I think this is fair. Don't you?

"Legally speaking, if we leave the invitation unopened, say here on the mantel, then technically we can answer 'yes, we received it' without having to commit."

Avoiding Office Homework

I think at one time or another everyone has brought home work from the office packed in the old briefcase—which is then tossed on the chair in the front hall with a promise to "get at it" first thing Saturday morning.

Saturday morning rolls along and suddenly other matters of the weekend take priority. The kids need to be chauffeured to lessons. The grass needs a-cuttin'. The tool bench could use a cleanup. The dog, car and patio furniture all need to be washed. There's food to be bought. Etc., etc., etc.

Every so often you pass by the briefcase, vowing to get around to your homework first chance you get. When Sunday comes around there are golf games, extended family affairs, and of course the garage cannot go another day in its present state.

Throughout these two days you have managed to suppress any "guilt" attached to the responsibilities of work ... until about 11:00 Sunday night, when you can't stand it any more and you rip open your briefcase to reluctantly attack the task at hand.

You manage to finish by 3:00 a.m., just enough time to get about three hours of sleep. You arrive at the office to hear comment upon comment about "what a wild weekend" you look like you had, only to defend yourself by saying, "Not me. I worked the *entire* weekend on the big report due this morning." At which point you realize you were so tired when you left the house that you picked up junior's school bag.

How to Act When You Meet a Client

Have you ever been walking along, say, on Saturday morning on the waterfront, dressed in your sweats, looking unkempt, hangin' off your significant other, when suddenly you see somebody out of the corner of your eye and they are dressed equally "o-casual"?

You catch their eye and you can sense that they too are uneasy so you look away and keep walking. "Should I know this person? Was this an old lover I hurt?" Suddenly a light goes on.

"Oh my god! It's a client!" Or patient ... or any type of business associate with whom you have only a weekday relationship. It could even be your boss.

And for a moment you realize that you have never thought of this person as having a life other than the business world in which you know them.

Why do we think like this? I believe it goes back to grade one when we assumed that our teacher lived in the coatroom. And then were faced with the shocking reality of meeting her as she lay on the beach one weekend. (And we are not talking *Baywatch* material here.) This sight was too much for our brain, so from that day on we have always separated those who tell us to behave and those who want to party.

However, having witnessed someone hanging out of a thong bathing suit can be very beneficial to the dynamics of your weekday relationship.

Think about it.

"Oh my god! It's Larry Dawes, our biggest client. Just act naturally and whatever you do, don't look down."

Weekends Mean Responsibility Takes a Holiday

We live in a world of inconsistencies, hypocrisy and things that just don't add up. Take for instance the difference between what we'll put up with on weekdays and on weekends.

During the week we complain about morning rush-hour traffic jams, lineups at the bank, and the photocopier, while we yearn for the weekend when life seems less … rushed, packed and rigid.

Of course, we somehow manage to eliminate from our memory the bumper-to-bumper traffic out of the city on a Friday night, the two-and-a-half-hour wait to get into the latest special-effects movie on Saturday afternoon, or the three-hour Sunday lineup for a new theme-park ride that is guaranteed to make you upchuck.

So why do we spend our precious weekend time waiting like this? Well, the answer is quite obvious, isn't it?

It's the payoff. There's a pot of gold at the end of the line called mindless "fun." Fun. That's what we strive for on our weekends.

We are a generation striving to bring into our adult life the excitement of reading *Spider-Man*, going to summer camp, hanging ten or simply hanging out. We are a generation that will wait for an undetermined amount of time so that we can experience for even the shortest instant *no responsibility*. We are a generation that refuses to grow up.

And I count my blessings that we are, for otherwise I would not be the Weekend Guy. I'd probably be the Responsible Guy, talking about child-rearing, financial security and how to plan your own funeral … and *that* just wouldn't be fun.

Group of Seven ... The Next Generation

I'M STARVED. LET'S EAT!

Who Brought You Up? Weekend Kitchen Etiquette

Eating is a big part of any weekend experience, especially when you are away in the country. The air enhances one's appetite. Diets are abandoned. The actual preparation of a meal isn't a chore, it's an activity. Long gone are the days when the female of the species is stuck sweating away in a room all by her lonesome.

The kitchen is now a central focus of most retreats. Walls no longer exist, mentally or physically. Preparation stations are in vogue, to allow more than one person at a time to participate in making the meal. And of course cooking, especially at the weekend retreat, has crossed all sexual boundaries. Women do it. Men do it. Children do it … and *guests* do it.

As a guest, yes, you are on "holidays." But remember, so is your host! Some people, myself included, get off on taking charge and showing off their culinary talents. But just because you are told that everything is under control doesn't mean you can't help out. Part of being a good host is insisting that guests don't work. Part of being a good guest is insisting that you *do* work. In the end, a balance should be achieved.

If you are one of those people who claim that they do not know how to cook, there are still things you can do.

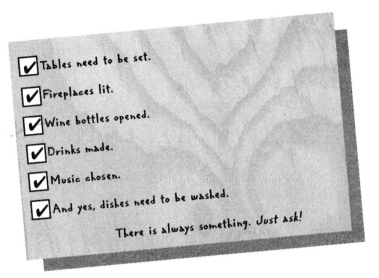

☑ Tables need to be set.

☑ Fireplaces lit.

☑ Wine bottles opened.

☑ Drinks made.

☑ Music chosen.

☑ And yes, dishes need to be washed.

There is always something. Just ask!

Bless Me Father ... A Word on Doing the Dishes

Over the years much discussion and debate went on over whether or not to get a dishwasher at the cottage. Mom always said that she preferred doing dishes by hand, and the thought of one more thing pouring waste into the septic tank drove my father nuts. This I could never figure out. Where did he think the water from the sink went? Personally, I believe my father, who still refers to the CD player as the phonograph, just couldn't see spending the money on what he believed to be a "luxury item."

Luxury? A dishwasher is a necessity. Washer and dryer at the cottage, *they* are a luxury. I mean, you can send your guests home with their dirty underwear, but you can't send them home with your dirty dishes.

So when I took over the cottage the first thing I did was to buy a dishwasher. This actually turned out to be a real eye-opener.

First, never have all the dishes used at any one weekend feast *ever* fit into one load. And second, I have come to realize that doing dishes at the cottage is a chance to relate on an interpersonal level, especially when you are entertaining a big crowd. It's something that anybody can do and, believe it or not, is a relaxing, mindless task that inspires deep conversation.

Doing the dishes on the weekend is like stepping into the confessional at church. You can say anything, and the other person is sworn to secrecy. You end up chatting about secrets, dreams and loves lost.

And why does this happen? Why is dishwater like truth serum? Is it the soothing warmth of the sudsy liquid? Is it the bonding that occurs because you are doing something in common? Nah. The answer is quite simple.

It's "'cause you're soaking in it."

Guys & Grills Come Out to Play

Okay, before I start, I just want to say that I am not a sexist. However, when it comes to the art of cooking over an open gas flame, also known as "BBQing," I think you have to agree that it is a guy thing.

It goes way back to the days when men went out, hunted dinner and brought it home to an open fire. Granted, women probably did the cooking while men probably acted out some hallucinogenic ritual fertility dance around the open pit dressed in brightly colored feathers. Still, the scent of the cooking fires has stayed with the male of the species through the eons.

Over the years, as we became more sophisticated, hunting was replaced by the supermarket and cooking moved inside, leaving this void in a guy's biorhythm. Until finally someone recognized men's natural urge to dress in loud colors and cook copious amounts of fatty red meat. So when suburbia was invented, and with it the backyard, some smart inventor named Ken took a cue from his wife Barbie, and the rest is history. The Barbie-cue was born.

Of course, in today's world, the thick three-inch slab of beef has often been replaced by the likes of grilled veggies and boneless breasts of chicken. And it is women who "act out" the charade of "playing dumb" when it comes to lighting the grill—be it charcoal or gas—allowing men to think they are still masters of their own little mystical ritual known as BBQing.

"It's his version of an extreme sport. He calls it the
light and dash!"

Bend Over and Cough! Giving the BBQ a Physical

Although BBQing is supposed to be somewhat informal, almost rustic, what it *isn't* supposed to be is rusty. I'm always amazed at the condition to which people allow their BBQs to degenerate. One friend of mine used to burn his eyebrows off every time he lit his rusty old contraption. He corrected this problem by getting longer matches.

I suggest you give your BBQ a checkup way before allowing it to get this bad. Believe me, your eyebrows will thank you.

Dealing with Freeloaders

Did you know that owning a gas BBQ is like being a landlord? No, I'm not referring to your freeloading brother-in-law.

When you haul the BBQ out of winter storage, before connecting the gas tank remove the burner located under the grill and lava rocks. You'll notice it has a set of tail pipes or venturi tubes. Spiders love to set up house here and interfere with the flow of gas. This area can easily be cleaned out using pipe cleaners or a pliable "venturi" brush, available at your local hardware store.

Checking for Leaks

Turn the tank, but not the controls, on.

The best method to check for gas leaks is to take some soapy water and drip it over all the connections. If gas is leaking, the water will bubble up.

Also, check the pliable gas tubes. Excessive drying due to age or exposure to cold or sun may cause the rubber to crack. If there are any serious cracks, replace the tubes. *Don't* try repairing them with duct tape—one person I know did and is lucky to be alive. Also, it's good to apply vinyl cleaner once a season. This reduces the effects of sun exposure and keeps the tubes flexible.

No Tanks

I'm not one for government intervention, especially when it comes to how I enjoy my weekends. However, sometimes people just need to be whipped. Just as a reminder. Like when it comes to propane gas tanks.

I love watching what people expect the poor kid at the gas station to fill up. Rusty, deteriorating pieces of junk they call tanks.

Now all tanks are dated and supposed to be disposed of after a set amount of time, depending on where you live. However, this alone is not a cure for stupidity. Will it kill you to take a can of rust paint and give your tank a little spritz every few years? Not only will it look better, but this slows down the rust and reduces any possibilities of future leaks.

Weekend Guy Tip:

☞ An easy way of checking the fuel in your gas tank is to simply mist the side with cool water. A line will appear indicating the amount of gas left.

A Weekender's Diet Plan

What is it about weekends that make us turn off the right side of our brain, especially when it comes to eating?

For some reason we believe that calories also have the days off. We'll eat skinless breast of chicken during the week but throw a two-inch hunk of red meat onto the barbie on Saturday night. Never touch dessert Monday to Friday but down half the chocolate mousse from the sweets table at a wedding. Or snack on plain bran muffins each morning at the office but think nothing of wolfing down pizza, beer, pretzels and a couple of dogs up at the lake.

And what's our excuse? *It's the weekend!*

Weekends give us permission to let go, cast fate to the wind and live like there is no tomorrow. Weekends are for living life to excess! Because we know that come Monday morning there is always the gym, along with work-related stress, to help us get back on the diet wagon.

THE WEEKEND DICTIONARY

FRIDGE (n.) frhi–dʃeh

One of the biggest mysteries in any cottage or cabin, the fridge is the greatest magic trick ever seen. Known for its mysterious ability to devour hundreds of dollars worth of groceries in a single weekend, the fridge is also the sight of many famous archaeological digs. It has been the final resting place of many ancient bottles of mustard, ketchup and mayonnaise. Still, even after all these years, no one has claimed to have discovered the rarest of all finds ... the leftover bottle of beer!

But, Do You Dare Open It?

The refrigerator can be one of the scariest things.

By the end of the summer it not only acquires its own taste, it also learns to multiply. One year during the annual cleanout up at the cottage I counted six bottles of mustard, three huge mega-containers of ketchup, umpteen bottles of sweet, corn and hot relish, four mayos, a couple of half-full containers of salsa, and three liter-size containers of expired coffee cream. And this was just on the top shelf!

How does this happen? Well, it's not me. To be honest, besides coffee cream, usually in small quantities, I never purchase any of the above condiments. It's guests, usually the lazy ones. You know the type. Their idea of shopping for food when visiting the cottage is bringing along the institutional-size ketchup they picked up at the Price Club.

We interrupt this book with an important note from the author …

Okay, all you guests staying at someone's place this weekend, I speak for your host when I say that unless you plan on eating a bowl of mustard for dinner, condiments *do not count* when you say you are going to take care of a meal. Steak, salmon, even pasta—*that* counts as a meal. Not ketchup.

We now return you to our regular reading.

"Here, I brought you this. It was going bad
in my fridge at home."

TIME OUT

Time seems to be irrelevant when it comes to eating at a weekend retreat, unless of course there are either very young or elderly people in attendance, who seem to dictate the schedule more.

Generally, though, the clock stops ticking on the weekend and people like to eat when they get hungry … which seems like most of the time. So it's important that you create foods that can be made in advance or quickly assembled.

Now, here are two ideas for the great weekend munchies: the All-In-One Sandwich and BBQ Pizza. Both are simple, can be prepared in advance, will impress the hell out of your guests and begin with my nana's good old-fashioned pizza dough.

The Eighth Wonder: Nana's Pizza Dough

Actually, crediting my nana with this recipe is taking liberties. It's very common. Of course, you may notice that I'm not saying *which* grandmother to whom I am referring. Maybe it's Nana Grittani or maybe Nana Farano. The only real difference between their pizza was … well, quite frankly, Nana Grittani had this habit of burning everything she baked. To her credit we always believed it was the oven and that she was too frugal to get it fixed.

So to give them both equal time, let's just say Nana Farano inspired the dough and Nana Grittani was the inspiration for BBQing pizza.

Ma, you buy that, don't ya?

Nana's Pizza Dough

Ingredients:

3 cups all-purpose flour
1 tsp sugar
1 1/2 cups lukewarm water

1 pkg yeast
pinch of salt
olive oil

Begin by putting 3/4 cup of lukewarm water into a small bowl, and dissolve into it 1 teaspoon of sugar and 1 package of yeast. Let sit for 5 minutes until foamy.

In a large bowl or food processor (both nanas would turn in their graves if they saw me using a machine rather than my hands) mix flour, activated yeast, pinch of salt, 3/4 cup of remaining water, and a tablespoon of olive oil. Knead until smooth.

Place the dough into another large, oiled bowl, cover with a tea towel and place in warm area. In one hour punch down the risen dough and let it rise again!

The All-In-One Sandwich

Ingredients:

Nana's Pizza Dough

1 zucchini sliced lengthways

1 large tomato

large mushrooms thinly sliced

salami or ham

1 green pepper

olive oil

1 red pepper

chopped basil

sundried tomatoes soaked and drained

1 eggplant sliced into quarter-inch
pieces and sweated with salt

mozzarella cheese

parmesan cheese

Grill sweated eggplant, zucchini and peppers on the BBQ, remembering to baste with olive oil.

After Nana's dough has risen for a second time, roll it out on a floured surface into a circle with a 20-inch diameter. Lift the dough and line a greased 10-inch spring pan, allowing the excess (about 3 inches) to hang over the ends.

Place a layer of grilled eggplant on the bottom of the pan, then start layering with everything until packed to the top, seasoning and sprinkling with cheese as you go along.

Fold over the extra dough and seal with olive oil.

Bake at 350 degrees for 45 minutes.

Let cool, remove from spring pan and cut like a cake.

The result is a dish that looks more difficult than it is to make, and impresses the hell out of your guests.

The All-In-One Sandwich

The All-In-One is the perfect weekend retreat sandwich. I also call it the Super Bowl Sandwich. Actually, it knows no season or location and can be served either hot or cold. It can also be altered according to special diets and needs.

BBQ Pizza!

For years I tried to get my dear friend Sally Smith, caterer to the stars in L.A., to come up and visit me at the cottage in Muskoka. Finally, last summer, she and her husband George managed to clear some time and show up at the lake. Not only was I excited to see them but I knew Sally would take over the kitchen and pass on a few of her latest treats.

Unfortunately, she had to cut the visit short, for Joel Schumacher decided to throw an impromptu birthday party for himself with Tom, Nicole, and Arnold ya-di-da-di-da (how's that for name dropping?). However, before she left Sally did manage to pass on an idea that is simple and trendy to boot. Wonderful, crispy, thin pizza that resembles the taste of stone-oven baked but requires just the BBQ.

First, rather than repeat myself, I'll refer you to my nana's earlier pizza-dough recipe. But this time allow the dough to rise only *once*.

When you are ready to eat, gas up the old barbie on high. Get it good and hot. Meanwhile, take a small ball of dough and on a well-floured board roll it out flat, to less than a quarter-inch thickness. Now, flour your hands and slide them under the dough.

Next, yell out for someone to get the door and open the BBQ lid quickly. Lay the dough directly onto the grill and close the lid for about one minute. Then open the BBQ: you should discover a big bubble. Pierce it with a knife and flatten with a spatula. Check to see that the dough is not burning. When brown, lift the pizza from the grill and place back on the floured board, with the uncooked side faced down.

Now repeat with the rest of dough until you have baked as many as you need, on one side only.

Dress each pizza with sauce, cheese, and other favorites. Lower the BBQ flame to medium. Bake the pizza on the grill until the cheese is melted and the bottom is lightly browned.

Prepare for a taste sensation.

So Explain to Me, Why Do We Have Canine Teeth?

For all you vegetarians out there, now is a good time to flip the page, 'cause I'm talking beef. More specifically, BBQing a steak.

I assume if you are still reading this that you do partake in the deed.

- The first thing to remember is that all steaks are not created equal. Thick edges of fat do nothing but cause flareup. I always trim most of it off and score the remainder every inch or so. I like my steaks marbled, meaning having some veins of fat throughout, usually T-bones or New York cuts. Leaner cuts like flank, round and London broiled are best marinated overnight.

- The time for cooking a steak is a matter of preference. However, the method is the same. No matter what cut you are grilling, the steak should be removed from the refrigerator and brought to room temperature before being tossed on the flame; otherwise it may not cook as evenly as you would like, and this can even affect the taste.

- Second, you want to cook over a hot, preheated grill.

- I always rub the steak with olive oil, then quickly sear it on both sides at high. Then I reduce the heat slightly, turning once and cooking it until it's the way I or my guests like it.

- Generally, aged, marbled steaks cook a lot quicker than fresh, leaner cuts.

How do you spice it? That I'll leave up to you. Just remember, you're eating a steak to enjoy it, not because you have to, so don't bury the taste.

I Wish They All Could Be California Grills!

Now it wouldn't be right to talk about BBQs without passing on one of my weekend BBQ sauce recipes that is so easy to prepare that even your brother, who burns water, will be able to impress not only himself but his entire family.

I realize that there are some good prepared sauces out there on the market, but there's nothing like a fine homemade one. Not only is it tasty but for all you Martha Stewart wannabes, homemade BBQ sauce with your own personal label makes a great gift to present to hosts—and for hosts to present to guests.

The Weekend Guy's Famous Head for the Hills Hotter than Hell BBQ Sauce

This is especially great for a mess-o-ribs feast. Makes 4 cups.

Ingredients:	
4 tbsp vegetable oil	1 cup chopped onions
4 tbsp minced garlic	1/2 tbsp cayenne pepper
2 tsp cumin	1 tbsp Dijon mustard
2 cups ketchup	1/2 cup malt vinegar
1/2 cup red sherry or vermouth	1/2 cup soya sauce
1/2 cup dark brown sugar	4 tbsp Worcester sauce
Tabasco sauce and chilis to taste	

Heat oil in medium-size saucepan. Add onions, mustard, garlic, cumin and cayenne. Sauté over medium heat for 5 minutes. Stir in remaining ingredients and simmer. Continue to stir until thick (about 10 min.). Let cool, then bottle in fancy-shmancy bottles.

Label and give with pride.

Grilling Chicken on the BBQ

There is nothing like BBQ chicken. There is also nothing like chicken that hasn't been grilled properly. Yuk! Okay, here are the most important things to remember when BBQing this popular bird.

- First, all parts of the chicken are not the same. The darker meat, like legs and back, will take longer to cook than the white meat of the breast.

- Second, when you are cooking with the bone and skin still on, the first thing to do is to sear the piece, skin-side down, over a high heat, then flip it and cook on a covered grill over a medium heat until the meat near the bone is opaque and juices near joints run yellow with a tiny trace of pink when pierced. If you are in a hurry, you may try quickly microwaving your pieces first. This will start cooking the meat near the bone.

- Here's one of the most common mistakes I see people making. If you are using BBQ sauce—and I am talking sauce not marinade here—apply it only toward the end of the cooking process. If you put it on at the beginning, by the time the inside is cooked the sauce, which usually contains sugar of some sort, is burnt to a crisp. BBQ sauce is meant to add flavor to the outside, not to penetrate throughout.

Following these simple steps will make BBQing chicken your specialty.

BBQ Marinade

Very often a BBQ recipe calls for marinating. Whereas most foods taste great on the grill just the way they are, for others proper marinating beforehand is essential, especially for lean types of beef, fish and game.

Marinades are usually made up of three basic ingredients:

- Acidic-based ingredients like vinegar, citrus, soy sauce, wine and tomatoes are used to tenderize tough meats like flank steaks.

- Oil helps to moisturize the meat.

- Flavorings like sugar, honey and herbs: they are self-explanatory.

One big question that is always asked when it comes to marinating is, how long do you leave the beef or fish sitting in the mixture? Well, the general rule is that fish should never marinate more than 30 minutes, so as not to overpower its natural taste. On the other end of the scale, strong gamey meats like venison can be marinated overnight. While marinating you should always keep the foods well chilled in the refrigerator—and never pull it right from the fridge and onto the grill.

BBQ Peppers

Grilled marinated peppers ... To be honest, I don't know who to credit for this one. It's something I've known all my life as basically just another one of those great Italian recipes that work on the barbie. I will say this, though ... in Ontario, peppers, like so many of the great vegetables, have a season and are cheapest obviously in the fall. So if you have the time one weekend in September, buy a bushel of peppers and do a whole batch. You can jar this recipe and have it on hand for later.

Cover the grate of a hot BBQ with whole peppers. Close the lid and leave until the bottoms are burned and blistered. Rotate and continue to burn on all sides.

As you remove the peppers from the grill, drop them into a strong paper bag. Then fold over the top and leave in the sink. For the record, plastic does not work: you are steaming the skins off, so the bag needs to breathe—and also, plastic bags will melt.

After twenty minutes take out one pepper at a time and under cold water, using just your fingers, remove the skins and seeds. What remains should resemble a piece of salmon fillet.

Dry on a paper towel, cut into strips and place in a bowl. When all peppers are stripped, pour a mixture of olive oil, a touch of vinegar, garlic (the more the merrier), salt, pepper, fresh basil and parsley over them. Mix well, cover and refrigerate.

Remove from fridge half an hour before you are ready to eat, and serve on a plate with small pieces of bread toasted with olive oil and oregano.

Keep remaining peppers in jars. Unless you sterilize and properly seal the containers, you must keep the peppers refrigerated.

BBQ Eggplant

BBQ garlic eggplant spread. It's really simple and again is the type of recipe that impresses guests.

Place a large eggplant, or for pretentious people "aubergine," onto a hot grill, pierce it with a fork, and close the cover. You must remember to pierce it or else you'll be scraping mush from everywhere inside your BBQ. I speak from experience.

Cook the eggplant until it deflates and the inside is really soft. Remove from the grill and allow to cool until you are able to handle it without burning yourself. Again, I speak from experience.

Scoop the insides out and place into a food processor.

Add:

2 tbsp olive oil	1/4 cup pine nuts
4 large cloves peeled garlic	a shot of soya sauce
1 peeled, seeded and chopped tomato	chopped parsley
1/4 cup raisins	

Pulsate until medium smooth.

Place the mixture into serving bowl, cover and refrigerate for a couple of hours. Actually, I find that this spread always tastes better the next day. It allows for all the wonderful tastes to blend.

Remove mixture half an hour before you are ready to serve. In the meantime, take a baguette and cut into thin slices. Place them on a cookie tray, brush with a mixture of olive oil and minced garlic.

Toast on the BBQ or in the oven.

Spread with the eggplant and enjoy a heavenly treat.

Drunken King Tut

I first presented this on Cottage Life Television and it is my most requested recipe. The best thing about this is that you get to clean out the refrigerator at the same time. Literally. Old veggies and fruits are perfect. Nothing is wasted.

"Show me the way to de-bone ..."

You'll need:

1 big mother of a turkey	everything but the kitchen sink
1 cup garlic butter	salt
lemons	paprika
celery stalks	pepper
apples	1/2 cup vodka
oranges	1/2 cup orange juice
onions	large cheesecloth
carrots	toothpicks
garlic cloves	large roasting pan

Wash and dry the turkey. Peel several cloves of garlic and rub over inner and outer skin of turkey, then place the cloves into roasting pan. Cut and peel apples, oranges, celery, carrots (etc.) placing their peelings and leaves into pan. Then stuff the fruit or vegetables into the turkey cavity. Lay a double layer of cheesecloth over the pan, allowing the excess to hang over the sides. Place turkey in center of pan. Rub surface with 1/2 cup of garlic butter. Season to taste. Fold cheesecloth over top and secure with toothpicks. Spread remaining garlic butter over the top of cloth. Mix orange juice and vodka and pour half the mixture over the cloth. Cook in preheated oven at 350 degrees, for 20 minutes per pound. Halfway through cooking, pour remaining juice mixture over top, keeping cloth moist. Don't scream when you open the door the second time. The bird will look burnt to a crisp. When done (use thermometer), remove, moisten cloth with mixture and let sit for 20 minutes. With scissors, begin at one end and carefully remove the cheesecloth. Be prepared to be amazed! Better still, make sure your guests are present at the unveiling ... you'll look soooo good, baby.

Variation on a Theme ... Cranberry Marinade

Whichever way you choose to cook your turkey, you may want to try
marinating it first overnight.

Mix:

2 cups cranberry juice cocktail

2 tsp salt

1/2 cup orange juice

1/2 cup olive oil

2 tsp pepper

1/2 cup fresh cilantro

Place turkey in plastic garbage bag; double-bag to be sure.

Pour liquid mixture in and seal tight.

Turn several times and place in fridge overnight, turning every few
hours.

Discard marinade and bird is ready to cook!

A Side Issue ... Everyone Salsa!

Now, I've never been a big fan of stuffing, so look elsewhere for *that* recipe. However, owning a cottage near the town of Bala, Ontario, the cranberry capital of the world ... okay, Canada, I do like cranberries. But not in plain sauce, but rather *cranberry salsa*. This recipe makes the perfect gift item, and it ain't brain surgery to make.

Get out the old food processor and into it place ...

Everyone Salsa!
3 cups frozen cranberries
1/2 cup honey
2 tsp lime juice
1/2 cup chopped onions
2 fresh jalapeno peppers (seeded and chopped)
1/2 cup chopped dried apricots
1/2 cup fresh cilantro leaves
2 large chopped oranges
Pulse (chop) in processor until it forms a chunky mixture.
Refrigerate.
And that's it!

BBQ Turkey

Okay, by now you will probably realize that the BBQ is my favorite appliance, just as the chainsaw is my favorite tool. I will go to any lengths to BBQ turkey: rain, snow, hail, whatever! Maybe the picture of Mom lifting out the bird from the oven is engraved in my memory.

To be honest with you, Mom's turkey was always an itsy-bitsy bit too dry. This is something that I learned only later in life, when I discovered what a difference a BBQ makes. First, unlike electric heat, gas is moist—and in a closed BBQ the air circulates, creating a convection-like atmosphere.

Then, of course, there are several new BBQs with a rear flame that, when combined with a rotisserie, is simply heaven. Because the flames are to the side, you can place a pan underneath to catch the drippings.

However, for those whose BBQ does not have a rotisserie or rear flame, it is still possible to BBQ the bird by placing the turkey into an aluminum disposable pan. Then take another pan and spread small pebbles on the bottom.

Pour 1 cup of either water, beer or white wine over the pebbles. Then place the pan with the prepared seasoned turkey inside. Cover with foil, shiny side in, and place on the grill to cook (20 minutes for each pound).

Baste as needed and replenish the liquid in the lower pan when required. Remove the foil for the last 15 minutes. You may find that it takes less or more time, depending on the individual BBQ. However, generally I find the bird will cook a lot faster than in a conventional oven.

Grilling Seafood

If you do nothing but cook burgers on your BBQ, maybe it's time to experiment and move on to something else, like grilled seafood. Although the types of seafood available for grilling vary according to location and season, the basic methods remain the same.

If you like grilling whole fish, I suggest you invest in a hinged wire fish basket, which helps to turn the fish without it falling into pieces. If you are cooking directly on the grill it's best to oil the surface first and turn the fish only once. This goes for fillets and steaks as well. And always cook with the skin on to retain moisture and keep it together.

Marinating fish isn't like marinating beef. It only takes about 30 minutes maximum; otherwise the flavor of the marinade can take over and you might as well be eating tofu.

One thing to stay away from when grilling fish is seasoning with salt. The salt draws out moisture and turns your fish into cornflakes.

Steaks and fillets are best grilled over a high, direct flame and larger whole fish over an indirect flame. You can plan for about 10 minutes per inch of thickness for all fish. *Remember, fish cooks quickly*—and keep in mind that fish continues to cook even after it is removed from the grill.

The Art of Serving Beer

To me the whole beer phenomenon reminds me of the NHL. I remember when I was a kid, it used to be six teams, six brands of beer. Then came the expansion. Now there are too many teams to keep track of and the same goes for the beer. Dark, pale, iced, strong, high alcoholic content ... and the same goes for beer.

With all the effort you put into choosing a beer, why not go one step further by properly storing and serving your choice?

For instance, all beer should be kept in a cool dark area in an upright position. And once you refrigerate beer, keep it there or on ice until serving.

If you are having a party it's best to chill beer in batches, so you don't end up having to remove remaining bottles to make room for leftover food. Beer will lose its taste with excessive cooling and warming. Unpasteurized beer should always be refrigerated and drunk within one to two weeks.

Finally, beer is always best served in large chilled glasses. Even if you are using plastic glasses at a party, keep them in the fridge and remove as needed.

And as with the NHL, choosing a winning beer is like choosing a winning team: Canadians do it best.

Blah! Blah! Blah! Dinner Talk, a Low-Calorie Appetizer

Dinner on the weekend is always an event. With our schedules today, it's most likely the one time that families and friends get the opportunity to sit down and have an actual conversation.

A dinner in the country is no exception. As a matter of fact, it seems to bring out the closeted politician, religious fanatic, opinionated bourgeois, righteous leftist and left-handed rightwinger in all of us.

I'm not sure if it's the fresh air, the natural surroundings or the casual dress, but I've watched married couples argue, children confess and the meek become lions. All at the dinner table on the weekend.

However, sometimes conversation *does* need a boost, change of subject or just a simple starter, especially at weekend retreats where the invited guests are meeting for the first time.

At my place I keep a jar in which I store pieces of paper with questions written upon them. When the need arises I order someone to pull out a question and answer it. Sometimes it can be in the middle of an argument or discussion. Sometimes I use the questions simply as appetizers.

Of course, the outcome will depend on a person's honesty, their integrity and their desire to get a return invitation.

Here is a sample of the questions in my jar. For your convenience I've categorized them by their expected response:

Pleasant Chit-Chat.

- How long did it take for you to get here?
- What wildlife have you seen this weekend?
- What was the first thing you did when you arrived?
- What new thing did you learn about your hosts?
- How would you describe the view?

- How many times have you been here before and what changes in your life have been made since your last visit?
- What was the biggest surprise about this visit so far?
- If you could have brought along a celebrity, who would it have been?
- In one word, describe how you felt when you arrived.
- Admit it. Did you overpack?

Stimulating Dialogue.
- What was the reason for this visit?
- If this weekend was a book, who would the author be?
- Look around. Describe what you see.
- What will always make you smile when you remember this weekend?
- What event this weekend do you wish you had captured on film?
- If you weren't here what would you be doing?
- What games were played (either board or mind)?
- What would you love to steal from this place?
- What is the most memorable taste from this weekend so far?
- Give all the details of a dream you have had since you arrived.

Energizing Discussion.
- If this was your place, what would you change?
- If this weekend was a movie, what would its title be and who would play you?
- Admit it. Did you come here to please or to be pleased?
- What was the one thing you did this weekend to reduce your guilt and earn your keep?

- Describe your host's sense of style … or lack of.
- In a week's time, what will you remember most about this weekend?
- How long did it take for you to get this invitation?
- What was the funniest thing that happened this weekend?
- What was the defining "smell" of the weekend?
- What one word best describes you as a guest?

All-Out Knock-Down Debate.

- What is the biggest contribution you have made to this visit?
- As a guest, rate your host from 1–10. As a host, what one word describes each guest?
- What tip would you like to pass on to your host?
- The only thing wrong with this visit was that there wasn't enough _____.
- Who is the center of gossip this weekend?
- What did you do for the first time this weekend?
- What is the best excuse you can make up to extend your visit?
- Describe how you feel about leaving.
- What promise would you make in order to get invited back?
- How did you sleep and how was your bed?

Planning Your Own Weekend-Themed Video Festival

It's amazing how within relatively few years watching a video or two on the weekend has become a tradition up at the lake. So why not embrace this activity with open arms and plan an entire weekend—by creating your own video festival the next time a whole gang is coming up to visit?

"Honestly! Just once I'd like to rent a video one Saturday night where you stay awake and I don't have to explain how it ended."

The easiest way to organize this event is to choose a *theme*—for which guests have to provide the flick. Take it one step further and get them to prepare a *theme meal* along with it, like pasta for a spaghetti western or oysters for a romantic comedy. You can even get a group of neighbors together and take turns hosting a different meal and film. The possibilities are endless.

So next time, rather than just rent any video that happens to be available, why not put a little planning into the activity and turn it into an annual event?

ALL I EVER DO IS ...

The Difference Between a Job & a Chore

What's the difference between a job and a chore? You work your butt off all week long and you get paid for it. That's called "a job." Then the weekend comes and suddenly you find yourself raking the leaves, cutting the lawn, finishing the rec room in the basement, building a dock and painting the kid's bedroom while packing the freezer with a week's worth of dinners. These are called "chores."

The difference between a weekday job and a weekend chore is that one is work that they tax, and the other can be a taxing situation that is work.

Tooling Around

Men and their power tools. I believe that when a guy puts a power tool in his hand a hormonal reaction occurs. There's a need to immediately try out the apparatus. Beyond not reading the instructions, waaay beyond not even knowing what you call the thing, I know guys who plug it in, rev it up and attempt to use the machine without even a hint of knowing what the thingamajig was designed to do. This is *definitely* a guy thing.

Women approach power apparati in an entirely different manner. First of all, if it's new, they remove the tool from the box like they are performing a vasectomy, and immediately they go right to the instructions and read them from A to Z, in English and in French and in Italian and in German and in Japanese.

Then they go out and buy the extended manual.

Then they take the continuing education course, which is followed by subscribing to the magazine and watching the specialty channel dedicated to how this tool can enhance their entire life.

And finally, while women will store the tool back in its original box, a guy, when the five-minute attention span expires, will go inside, open a beer, turn on the game and leave the spanking brand-new tool outside to rust in the rain—and will never think about it again until the next golf tournament, where he will win the exact same tool, rip open the box, plug it in and rev it up!

The Chainsaw

I find it strange that the most lethal thing at one's weekend retreat is not licensed. No, I am not talking about your mother-in-law, I'm referring to the chainsaw.

I'm always amazed when I catch people out there sawing a tree down without using any precautions. One should never even *look* at a chainsaw without first slipping into a pair of steel-toed boots, easy-to-move-in leather gloves, a hardhat and safety glasses.

If you don't have a chainsaw but are planning on buying one and trying to figure out what size to purchase, a sixteen-inch blade is more than adequate for the average weekender.

I recommend that unless you have used one before, in addition to reading the manual thoroughly you get someone with experience to show you how to operate it and fell a tree. And as far as maintenance is concerned, the two most important rules are ...

- Always check to see that you have enough chainsaw oil.

- Never, never, never let the chain touch the ground. This will ensure that you will always stay sharp and on all of your toes.

"It's not how easily it takes the tree down but rather how it takes their testosterone level up that amazes me."

Choosing a Woodstove

Did you know that today when you buy a woodstove you're also purchasing a gas one?

Because all wood releases gas when burned, if your stove is not designed to be airtight and doesn't allow the temperature to build so that these secondary gases are burned off, flammable creosol forms on the inside wall of your chimney and could result in a fire.

However, today's modern woodstoves are designed to be more than just pretty fixtures in the corner of a room. They are airtight, and much of the gas from burning wood is forced back through the fire box to burn off. This increases the unit's overall efficiency. If you also install *insulated* stove pipes, any gas that does manage to make it through is less likely to cool and crystallize.

When buying a new woodstove, don't purchase one that is designed to heat a space larger than what you require. This can actually lower the efficiency of the unit. Make sure that you know the measurements of the room or rooms you are planing to heat.

In addition, it's important that you always burn dry, hard woods like maple and avoid soft pulpy species like cedar, which create even more gas when combustion occurs.

However, whether you install a new high-efficiency unit or already have an older woodstove it is important that the chimney is cleaned at least once a year whether you burn for a source of heat or simply romantic ambience.

Chim-Chimmery

I'm always amazed at the number of people who have used their fireplaces for years and yet have never even thought of cleaning out the stack.

I'm talking specifically about people who still believe that a fireplace is for burning wood, not gas, or who have a lightbulb with a little flickering thing spinning around on top. And why exactly does one have to clean the chimney? It has nothing to do with aesthetics. It has everything to do with safety and preventing chimney fires.

Two common reason for fires in the chimney are blockage, like animal and bird nests, or a buildup of creosol caused by cooling secondary gases emitted from burning wet or new wood. This creosol, a solidified form of the gas, can actually ignite and prove very dangerous in an older chimney.

How you clean the chimney is a matter of choice. Either have a professional do it, or if you are not afraid of heights purchase a proper chimney brush from your hardware store and do it yourself. In addition to the brush, I climb up on the roof and lower a long chain down the stack. A good shake knocks out any clumps attached to the sides. And if you are thinking that "I've gone this long, why bother," that's all the better reason to have it done. Do yourself a favor and get swept.

Or is that swept?

To Clean or Not to Clean. Is This a Question?

Unfortunately, for many of us, time on the weekend has to be set aside for household cleaning chores, even at the weekend retreat. Here are a few tips to help make the task more efficient.

✓ When cleaning windows, wipe the inside vertically and the outside horizontally. This way, if you make a streak, instead of wasting time running back and forth you'll know exactly which side it's on.

✓ Next, when cleaning out the fridge, don't forget to vacuum the dust bunnies clinging to the condenser on the back. This dust acts as insulation, making the unit work harder than it should.

✓ And finally, save the wood ashes from the fireplace. A mixture of ashes and a little water makes a great natural and non-toxic degreaser and cleaning abrasive on things like pots and fireplace doors.

The Ergonomics of Weekend Leisure

You hear a lot about ergonomics, the art of politically correct furniture design. These designs are supposed to be "good for you." But when it comes to good weekend furniture, ergonomics takes a back seat.

"Well, you know son, for some strange reason
he sets this trap for himself."

For instance, the hammock. Once you manage to get inside, your back is totally round and it gives you no support except to keep you off the ground, much like grandma's old bed up at the cottage. However, while it may not be good for you in the long run, a hammock immediately gratifies you with comfort.

When it comes to weekend clothing, design can again sometimes make way for comfort. Baggy and torn, stretched and worn—these may not be salable features at a retail level, but they do make for many a smiling weekend warrior.

I'm not saying there's no room for reason or aesthetics when it comes to enjoying oneself. It's just that my idea of making a good impression on the weekend is leaving my butt prints on the old feather and hay stuffed couch in front of a big stone fireplace in an old log cabin—hidden from anyone who cares what I look like.

Now *that's* comfortable weekend design.

Weekend Shopping ... Garage Sales

I find garage sales fascinating. I also find it interesting that the word garage is just garbage without the "b." I have seen people walk away from garage sales with crap that was probably there because it was refused by the previous week's garbage collection.

On the other hand, you can get some really nifty deals, depending on the situation of the person or persons selling the junk ... I mean, "merchandise."

Guys, look for sales conducted by a bitter divorced woman. Here you'll find power tools and sporting equipment, some still in the package, that she'll practically pay you to take out of her sight.

Also good is an estate sale where the surviving family members are feuding, making it very easy to play one against the other and practically walk away with a Louis XIV original.

But stay away from over-enthusiastic smiling couples whose names are Biff & Muffy, 'cause most likely they're trying to do to you what someone else has already done to them.

"I feel sorry for her. She had no idea what
a treasure she had."

Twig It!

So you've got that old end table or dresser. A real eyesore. It's nowhere near being an antique and about one step away from being firewood. However, you just can't bring yourself to do away with it. I say it's a prime candidate for a good twiggin'.

Here's how. Take a walk into the woods and collect three-foot-long twigs, half an inch in diameter. I prefer the look of birch. There's usually enough on the ground so you shouldn't have to cut anything down. At the same time, collect as many pieces of birch bark as you can carry, again from fallen trees.

Now, depending on the piece of furniture, you may want to throw on a coat of paint. Then, make like Martha Stewart and pull out the glue gun. Start attaching lengths of the twigs to the edges of the table. Then secure them with tiny finishing nails.

Take one-inch strips of birch bark and glue them on the surface to the inside edge of the twigs. Then finish the other edge with another line of twigs. You can either continue on with this pattern or stop. But whatever you choose, I guarantee your eyesore will become an eye catcher.

Exterior Painting Tips Avoid Doing It Next Year and the Next …

If painting the exterior of your home or cottage is on your weekend agenda, why not do it right the first time and avoid having to repeat the job next summer?

Properly done, a good exterior paint job should last for seven years. I hear many people blaming the paint when it starts peeling, when actually it was their method that was at fault.

The first thing is to make sure you are painting onto a clean, dry surface. One of the biggest reasons why paint peels is that the wood is wet. Either the wood was too new and still green, there's a seepage problem from behind or inside the building, or the painter was impatient and did not allow the first coat or primer to dry completely. Painting is not something you can rush. Take your time. Also, painting on a sunny hot day is not a good thing. The sun dries the paint too fast and can crack it or cause blisters.

So painting the exterior of your house or cottage is a slow, fair-weather process. Hmm, doesn't sound like the most exciting way to spend your weekend. But neither is the second attempt at it.

Dealing with Garbage

Anyone who has ever gone camping, or owns or rents a weekend retreat, knows that one of the biggest pains is dealing with garbage. Every weekend when it's time to go home it's the same ritual ... Deciding what to do with the garbage. You pay taxes but in many areas you don't get pickup. Sometimes I feel like just tossing the trash into the bushes. I mean, why else did they choose green as the color of garbage bags? However, thanks to my enviroguilt I would never do such a thing.

It would be nice if I could do what New York City tried a couple of years ago, and put the trash on a raft to let it float away. But I think the neighbors across the lake would probably not like this idea.

Leaving it behind the woodpile and dealing with it next week only encourages uninvited visitors ... *besides* in-laws.

So the only solution is to embrace the garbage, take it into your fold, and bring it back home ... so that someone hired by the city will ship it back out to a dump in the country.

Hey, we're talking politics here. You don't expect it to make sense, do ya?

Lawn Fetishism

I don't understand this obsession that we have with lawns. On any given weekend morning from May 'til September, you'll hear the BRRRRRM of lawnmowers off in the distance.

Every so often there's a loud NHHECK or CLANK when you run over Junior's lost skateboard wheel, or the dog's $25, supposedly indestructible chew toy. But still nothing stops us from trying to obtain the perfect lawn.

And what is the perfect lawn? A weedless plane of Kentucky blue that rivals the outfield at the SkyDome? The fairways of St. Andrews-by-the-Sea? Or how about the courts of Wimbledon?

Hmmm: baseball, golf and tennis.

What would I rather do? Cut the lawn or play?

I think the answer is obvious—but what we'd rather do is not always practical. Weekend after weekend can pass by and the baseball glove is fine just sittin' in the closet. The golf clubs will be okay in the trunk of the car, and the tennis racket won't warp in your locker down at the club.

However, by Monday those blades of chlorophyll have already begun plotting against you, racing with each other, growing at an unbelievable rate (and, if you listen carefully, even snickering at you) so that by Saturday morning when you are ready to hit the diamond, course or court, you are forced to cancel … because you are obsessed with having the perfect lawn.

The Dirt on Gardening

They claim that gardening has never been so popular.

Gone are the images of little old ladies down on all fours pruning their roses or plucking out weeds. Now the generation that

"It's not that I don't trust our financial advisor, but I figure our portfolio has a better chance of seeing growth here in the garden."

brought us macramé hanging pots filled with ferns is installing, not planting, gardens that are the envy of the grounds at the Palace of Versailles. Plants once native to exotic rainforests have found their way to the gardens and greenhouses of suburbia, or to city rooftops and balconies.

None of this behavior is surprising, for this is the same generation that *pruned* their lifestyle after a drought in the early nineties, that has seeded the *growth* of the mutual fund, and encouraged the *planting* of the cellular tower so that they can *uproot* themselves every weekend.

"Now that I've cut down all the trees it's amazing how I'm not being bugged by mosquitoes, animals and birds. Now I have the space to enjoy nature."

Landscaping Naturally

So you've got yourself a cottage, a hobby farm or maybe you are lucky and your home is located in a country setting. Simply heaven … except one day you notice that this heaven doesn't have any wildlife.

Somehow the fish aren't jumpin' near your shoreline since you ripped out those "yucky weeds" and laid down that prize-winning lawn. And you've noticed that squirrels, little chipmunks and birds don't come around since you cleaned up the forest floor and chopped down a couple of hundred trees 'cause you were feeling claustrophobic. The only things that *have* stuck around and multiplied are the bugs.

Attention class. Welcome to Environmental Landscaping 101.

First, you should landscape to complement what has taken millions of years to create. I don't care what anyone says—lawns and fertilizers don't belong at the cottage. Especially near shorelines. Think about building a longer dock beyond the weeds before ripping them up along the shoreline. The cribs of the docks will actually attract fish.

The floor of the forest isn't "dirty"—it's in transition and home to thousands of creatures. Bug-eating birds and bats will return if you leave some trees and shrubs for them to live and feed in.

In my opinion the best landscaping does not change the environment, but your own perspective.

Relax to the Max

Okay, picture this. Summer is half over and you still have not had a chance to relax. Sound familiar? That means you have either been constantly entertaining or working too much. Why not try taking a mini-vacation, without actually leaving?

First, surround yourself with a relaxing atmosphere. It's time to be alone. Get rid of the kids, husband, wife or whatever. I'll leave how up to you—just keep it legal.

Sound is important. Set the mood by experimenting with a few no-brainer, "new agey"-type CDs from artists like Michael Jones, David Lantz or William Ellwood, to mention a few of my favorites.

Fill the tub with hot water and your favorite aroma, one that reminds you of some place special. Eucalyptus foaming oil does it for me. Reminds me of traveling through the plush green hills of southern India.

Light a few candles and put on your favorite sunglasses, slip into the tub, then get lost in your mind. If this sounds too simple … it is.

Do yourself a favor. I'm telling you. No, I'm ordering you. Believe me, the world isn't going to stop just because you drop out for a day.

Relax.

Long Weekends

Ah, long weekends. Here's what I believe.

On the Monday of the week before, people are *already* gearing up. So if you're trying to do business during this time, you might have trouble—most people are trying to clear things from their desks and really don't give a damn. By the Thursday before the long weekend, you might as well join in the party.

Now, if the holiday is Friday, you *may* be able to make arrangements to do business by the following Tuesday—not Monday, 'cause that's recoup day. If the holiday is Monday, don't even *try* to do business afterward, 'cause Tuesday is then recoup day and Wednesday, although the second work day of the week, is next to Thursday, which is the official first day of the next weekend.

If this trend continues, by the new millennium *every* day will be a weekend and long weekends will become extinct. Now, Martha, *that's* a good thing!

"Daddy, is this why they call it a long weekend?"

GET UP & GOOOOOOO

The Weekend Warrior

There are many signs of a true weekend warrior. Even though back at the office one may wear three-piece executive armor to hide the results of a weekend lifestyle, a business suit cannot disguise the wounds of one who, outside the confinement of glass and steel, has been vulnerable to the elements.

The way one easily settles back into the office chair can signify a back covered with bites, or scorched by the rays of an intrusive sun.

The way one limps down the hall in $300 designer shoes may indicate a nail that pierced the "sole" of a backyard do-it-yourselfer, or a hamstring pulled when that lonely suicide peak challenged the aging snow buff.

When asked, the true weekend warrior is proud to relay the story, and not above embellishing the challenge with a little bit more height, speed or magnitude.

For true weekend warriors know no defeat.

Tuning Up the Bike

Unless you are a courier in the city, biking is a seasonal weekend activity. In the spring, before you take out the old beast for its first run, I suggest giving it a quick tune up … the right way.

☞ The most common mistake? Over-oiling. Applying too much oil to the chain attracts dust and dirt and actually prevents the mechanism from moving smoothly. The best way to oil a chain is to apply the lubricant onto a sponge. Hold the sponge tightly around the chain as you turn the pedals. This method cleans it and applies just enough oil.

☞ Next, check your tires for any cracks that may have occurred over the winter. It's a good thing to wipe them with vinyl cleaner to keep them pliable.

☞ Check all brake pads and replace any that are smooth and treadless.

☞ And finally, before setting out, check your head. Don't forget, no matter how goofy you look or whatever it does to your hair, always wear a helmet. And make sure it fits properly. Not too big and not too small.

Choosing a B&B

One very popular way of experiencing the countryside these days is to check into a B&B. However, not all establishments are alike. Some B&Bs offer services comparable to a small luxury hotel—and they're just as exclusive. Some are like checking in with the Addams Family.

The best way to avoid disappointment is to call ahead. Most local tourist boards have a list of B&Bs in their area and are more then willing to mail or fax it to you.

Questions you will want to ask when phoning to inquire about a B&B:

☛ How long have they been in operation?

☛ What meals are included?

☛ What is the physical setup?

Some B&Bs are simply private homes, and you are sharing bathrooms, living rooms and dining facilities with the family—which can be very charming and a great way of learning about the local lore.

However, if you are looking for more privacy you may want to choose a B&B that has been set up in an old mansion, schoolhouse or converted country church, and where the host family has a separate area for themselves.

Either setup can be a very enjoyable and a memorable way of experiencing the local color.

"Well, we figured since Billy-Bob got married his bed
was just sittin' here, and since ma's up at 4:00 a.m.
cookin' anyway, why not start a B & B?"

"Like, how full do you want it, dude? Your firstborn,
your soul or an indecent proposal to your wife?"

SMACKIN' WAVES:
WEEKEND WATERCRAFTS

Buying a New Powerboat

So you want to buy a new powerboat and you have no idea where to begin. I say begin in your head, before you even look at your first craft.

Think first about *why* you are buying the boat. Is it *for* the cottage or *is* it your cottage? Will you be the only one driving it or will it be shared by many? Do you need power for pulling skiers or will the boat be used mostly for taking guests out on tours of the lake?

Finally, consider the issue of space. Do you need the boat for chores, like carting luggage and supplies to an island property? Or do you need to be able to safely cast your fishing rod without hooking a passenger?

You may notice I haven't even begun to ask about money, your experience and finally, style. It's funny, I think—sexy styling is what attracts people to a lot of boats ... which results in them buying crafts too big for their lake and budget, or too powerful for them to handle.

I'm not saying there's anything wrong with wanting to look good. But besides looking good, you should feel in control, and even consider taking a powerboating course before you launch the craft.

Buying a new powerboat should be an investment—not a mistake.

Buying a Used Boat

Since I have watched my father over the years buy one used lemon, I mean powerboat, after another, I feel like an expert, at least from an observer's point of view, on what to look for when buying a used craft.

First, if you are buying it while in the water you might as well phone in your offer. Inspect the boat *out* of the water. Look for cracks in the hull above and below the waterline. Investigate anything over one inch thoroughly. Try pressing your hands on different areas over the hull. If it flexes, that's not a good thing. Lift up any carpets and check under them for rot. A loose seat usually means either a loose screw or that there's nothing to screw into.

As far as the engine is concerned, now is the time to check the boat in the water. You're looking for a smooth start that maintains itself at all speeds. Clanks and grinding sounds during gear shifts should send up a flag. The battery and cables should be secure and clean. Play with all the buttons to make sure pumps pump and lights light.

What's all this matter in the end? Not much, 'cause most people still buy boats by the way they look ... Which is why you should take along a friend who really knows boats.

Personal Watercraft

Guess what? Personal watercraft are no longer a fad. They are a fact of life. Big time. And here to stay. I must commend the industry for listening to suggestions and working at improving standards, especially reducing the noise level. However, when it comes to personal watercraft safety, it is the driver, not the machine, that still needs tuning up.

For some reason there are people out there that think they are oblivious to all the rules of the water. You are a boat, not a toy, and subject to all the same rules, even a few more ...

I love riding a PWC and right now I am enjoying the freedom of self-regulation. So drive smart, which includes driving sober.

"I don't understand why they call them personal if I'm the one that hears 'em, sees 'em and is annoyed by 'em!"

PWC Tips:
- You must wear a proper fitting, bright-colored life jacket.

- Speed limits and restrictions apply to PWCs as they do to all boats. Use common sense. Respect others. Keep a safe distance when riding the waves of larger boats. Your presence can make drivers nervous.

- Also, vary your play areas. Circling the same route, every day, in front of the same place, can be very annoying to those on shore.

Personal Flotation Devices

Everything in this world changes, including safety equipment—and usually for the better.

For instance, on the water it used to be that all you needed was a "life preserver" that you forced your head through and could use for everything from boating to water skiing to a butt saver in the canoe. Of course, when someone finally realized how useless these water-absorbing, cotton-covered, and difficult-to-move-in obstructions were, they invented the *personal flotation device* or PFD.

Okay people, they came up with PFDs for a reason. You may not like the bright red, yellow and orange colors they came up with, but when you are bobbing around in the middle of the lake and wondering why they can't spot you clinging onto that pale blue wiggly kid's swimming snake you threw in the boat 'cause you knew nothing would happen, you're going to regret it.

Look, don't be a cheapskate when it comes to saving yours and other's lives. Spend the money and get proper-fitting, approved PFDs.

And one size does not fit all, especially the kids.

"I know it floats, but I don't think a beer cooler qualifies as an approved flotation device."

WEEKEND HOBBIES

Always the Photographer

Are you the one forced to take every picture at a weekend event just because you remember to bring the camera? Are you the one too embarrassed to pick up your prints at the photo shop because they are sooo bad? Here are a few pointers that may turn you into a regular paparazzi!

Today's point and shoot cameras are supposed to be foolproof, and yet they can *still* produce lousy photos. That's because although they may be self-focusing and may tell you how much light there is in the room, they still don't set the scene. *You* do that.

I'm talking about more than just telling everybody to say cheese. You have to remember that you are the camera person and director, so when your subjects start yelling "take the picture," ignore them and take a moment to place people the way you want.

You can avoid those boring shots of Mom, Aunt Mary and Grandma sitting side by side on the couch by making one person stand, one sit on the arm of a chair and the other sit in the chair itself. A general rule is, if you draw a line between any three heads in a group you should form a triangle, resulting in a much more interesting shot.

When it comes to taking that "must have" photo at the dining room table, you can make Uncle Ted in the forefront look less like his head to too big for his body by standing up on a chair and shooting down on the group. Also, make sure no one is chewing food—it's not pretty.

And to avoid uninvited reflecting family ghosts, never shoot in front of a window, especially at night.

"For heaven's sake, Charlie, stop telling the bird to make love to your lens and just take the damn picture!"

For the Birds

You've all heard them, madly chirping away, trying to wake you up at the cottage or campsite. The birds.

I think we take birds for granted. They are like white noise: always in the background, and we really never take notice. Why not stop and take a closer look? Yes, I am suggesting bird watching.

I know—when you think of bird watching you think of stuffed shirts like Jane Hathaway from *The Beverly Hillbillies*. But searching and identifying birds is actually quite fun and calls upon your ability to be patient and agile. If you have a camera with a telephoto lens, it's a humane way of hunting that I call "shoot to still."

Getting started is easy. You'll need a decent pair of binoculars with a power of at least seven times fifty. This keeps you far enough away that you don't disturb your subjects but close enough to get a decent look.

Then you'll need a guidebook. You'll want one that isn't too general, that includes something of an in-depth study of species in your area, and that has great colored illustrations. And what's this going to do for you? Well, it'll probably relax you, educate you and best of all, it's a great excuse to get away from the in-laws when they visit. Happy birding.

"I don't care if Bob's your uncle. Tell that fish
if he doesn't end his meal break now he's going
to be the meal break!"

What We Really Need Is Another Fishing Show

Okay, I'm sure I'll get letters for this one. Fishing. I find watching it on television about as exciting as watching snooker. But I like going out on the lake and tossing a line once in a while. I don't consider fishing a sport—I think of it more as an activity, kinda like gambling. You win some, you lose some. Usually lose ... your temper, your hook, your lure, your line, and of course, the big one that got away.

But I don't understand why anyone would want to sit there in front of the TV, usually on the weekend, and watch someone *else* toss a line.

I think what peeves me the most is that these guys never get upset. They are always smiling. And they always catch a fish.

Hey, maybe I'd enjoy fishing more if I too had a production assistant standing there with a fish in a bucket, just in case they happen not to be biting that day. I consider that fake and far from real fishing.

Fore-Play: Why Golf Gets a Rise

What is the attraction about the game of golf?

There's a whole bunch of things influencing the fact that golf is one of the fastest growing sports. Yes, I play. I'm hooked and you know what? I don't even know why. I usually wanna quit after the first hole, and yet I continue.

"You gotta love that one. Can't even see it."

The game has these built-in features that seduce you, like if you screw up one hole there's always the next. So in a way, with every hole you get a clean slate and another try. It's like a new beginning.

The other thing is, unless you are on a PGA tour, no one is really looking and it's easy to forget a few swings ... Not that I ever do.

Yes, I think the number one reason for golf's rising popularity in this increasingly legal, politically correct, regulated, videotaping, drug testing, paparazzi, friends-taping you-and-turning-you-over-to-the-courts world we live in ... is that you can cheat and can get away with it 'cause no one gives a damn.

If You Can't Laugh at It ...

Most humor is based on two things. Fear and recognition. This is absolutely the case when it comes to weekenders. What do weekenders fear? Unexpected guests, unexpected costs and unexpected breakdowns. With this in mind, it's very easy to become a "funny weekender."

Here are a few starters.

Q: *Where do guests from hell sleep?*
A: On the septic bed.

Here the fear of being stuck with bad guests is, for lack of a better word, blended with septic humor. Now try this one.

Q: *What don't weekenders like to hear from their guests?*
A: "I brought you this. It was going bad in the fridge at home."

People with boats will appreciate …

> **Q:** *How does the marina guy say "Hello" in the spring?*
> **A:** "Here's your bill."

Or

> **Q:** *How does the marina guy say "Goodbye" at the end of the season?*
> **A:** "Here's your bill."

No matter where you weekend, the local governments love to see the city folk as a cash cow.

> **Q:** *Why is death easier to comprehend then paying taxes on a weekend retreat?*
> **A:** You have a better chance of understanding where your soul is going.

And the family, well it's an endless pool of chuckles …

> **Q:** *Why is a brother-in-law like a septic tank?*
> **A:** They both come back up when they are least wanted.

> **Q:** *How do you know when something needs to be fixed?*
> **A:** When your brother-in-law's back goes out.

Now you try it. Start with …

> **Q:** *How many guests does it take to change a lightbulb?*
> **A:** _____

Easy, ain't it!

A FINAL WORD

Popular Myth-conceptions

Over the years I have heard them all: folk tales surrounding cottages and other weekend retreats that I call "myth-conceptions." My favorite is that if you own a cottage then you must be *rich*.

Yes, there are some who inherited the lifestyle. However, the majority are working stiffs like you and me who, when they bought their weekend retreat, stopped eating in order to afford the place.

And then there are those who did inherit the place from their grandparents (who probably bought it with the spare change on the dresser 'cause it was cheap at the time). They too, when they are not fighting with their relatives, have stopped eating in order to pay the taxes.

Another myth about owning a weekend retreat is that it exists so you can *relax*. I wish. First, there are chores like unpacking, repairing the front porch, grocery shopping, fetching drinking water and the usual painting, gardening, mowing, wood chopping, twisting and turning. Then, if guests are coming, there's the extra bed making, cooking, general cleaning, more cooking and more cleaning.

Finally, when all is said and done there's the cleaning, packing, woodpile re-stacking, laundry and the toy and equipment storing.

Oh myth, so tell me—when do we relax?